THE NEW

Trust Your Intuition

SUPER

Predict Dangerous Situations

POWER

and Defend Yourself from the Unthinkable

FOR WOMEN

STEVE KARDIAN
with A. CLARA PISTEK

TOUCHSTONE
New York London Toronto Sydney New Delhi

Touchstone
An Imprint of Simon & Schuster, Inc.
1230 Avenue of the Americas
New York, NY 10020

First Touchstone trade paperback edition August 2017

TOUCHSTONE and colophon are registered trademarks of Simon & Schuster, Inc.

For information about special discounts for bulk purchases, please contact Simon & Schuster Special Sales at 1-866-506-1949 or business@simonandschuster.com.

The Simon & Schuster Speakers Bureau can bring authors to your live event. For more information or to book an event, contact the Simon & Schuster Speakers Bureau at 1-866-248-3049 or visit our website at www.simonspeakers.com.

Interior design by Jason Snyder

Manufactured in the United States of America

10 9 8 7 6 5 4 3 2 1

Library of Congress Cataloging-in-Publication Data is available.

ISBN 978-1-5011-5924-4
ISBN 978-1-5011-5925-1 (ebook)

To my wife and daughter

CONTENTS

■■■■■■■■■■■

FOREWORD

●●●●●●●●●●

When I was seventeen years old, I was kidnapped from a shopping mall in broad daylight, taken to an isolated location, and sexually assaulted.

I was in a parking lot, getting into my car after my shift at Woodfield Mall in a suburb of Chicago where I was working to pay for my upcoming college expenses. When I saw a man approaching me, all my internal alarms went off. He looked menacing and walked in an odd way. The parking lot was empty. It seemed that he was following me. I had an urge to run but ignored the messages my intuition was sending me, partly because I didn't know where to run and partly because I didn't want to cause a scene. I had been singing out loud and was embarrassed that he had heard me.

As I put my key into the lock of my car, a shadow came up behind me. Before I knew it, there was a knife at my throat and I was in the back seat of a car that was parked right across from mine. After I was assaulted, he drove me to a parking garage, set me free, and told me to count to one hundred while he made his getaway. During the time I was held captive and powerless, I managed to consciously catalog details about his car and face, and that information led to his later arrest. He was a repeat sex offender who was on parole for murdering a fifteen-year-old girl named Julie Angel.

That was twenty years ago, and the experience profoundly changed my life. I became a survivor activist and founded Promoting Awareness | Victim Empowerment (PAVE), a national nonprofit organization that helps to prevent sexual violence and empower survivors. When Steve Kardian heard my story, one of the first things he said to me was "You are lucky to be alive." I've learned that statistically, the chances of my surviving that experience and seeing my parents and family again were less than 5 percent.

The New Superpower for Women is a must-read for all women so that they will never have to hear the words "You are lucky to be alive." It is a must-read for all parents so that they will never have to go through what my mom and dad did.

All of Steve's passion for women's safety, his long history in law enforcement, which includes serving as an FBI defense tactics instructor, has been poured into this book. Using real-life scenarios, Steve explains what happens in the moments leading up to an assault and shows that how we respond in those seconds can affect our safety.

Although the perpetrator in my case was a stranger, overwhelmingly it is someone who we know and trust that commits the crime. This book arms us with concrete ways to protect ourselves in these situations as well. Steve also recognizes that crime is never the victim's fault. Especially in cases of sexual violence, survivors are often blamed and shamed into silence. Steve shatters the silence of sexual violence and equips us with the tools to better defend ourselves.

Shining a light on a culture that too often condones sexual assault and blames survivors, this book illuminates the key to unlocking every woman's superpower—trusting her own intuition.

Angela Rose
Founder and Executive Director of Promoting Awareness | Victim Empowerment (PAVE)
www.ShatteringTheSilence.org

INTRODUCTION

■ ■ ■ ■ ■ ■ ■ ■ ■ ■

The book you are holding is a straightforward and realistic guide to assessing predatory behavior before something bad happens to you. I will explain what criminals and predators look for when choosing a target and how you can master the cues your body language sends out so you give off an aura of strength and confidence. You will understand how to interpret seemingly random glances, how to recognize aggressive facial expressions, and how to react. I will also share how you can prepare yourself for any "worst-case" scenario, so that if you are threatened or find yourself in a dangerous situation, yes, you will be prepared.

Although crime can be random, a predator will take a few seconds to evaluate a potential target, and there you can control how you are perceived. It all starts with developing and trusting your intuition so that you can use it to anticipate trouble *before* it starts and prevent the unthinkable from happening to you.

I've spent more than thirty years in law enforcement, where I investigated thousands of crimes against women. During my inquiries and research, I found that in almost every case, a woman knew before she was attacked that something was not right. She could sense it, whether there was something about her attacker's attitude or his expression or the way he carried himself. Without being able to articulate why, women realized that the situation they were in was not good.

While all of us need to take precautions to stay safe, the truth is that crimes against women, along with their psychological, emotional, and physical effects, differ from crimes against men. The playing field may look the same, but it is a different game with different rules. When a predator attacks a man, the man's money or life, or both, are at stake. When a woman is attacked, her money or life, or both, are at stake, but there is also the real possibility for sexual violence.

The effects of a physical assault, an act that is purely about power and domination, can be devastating and take years to overcome. The predator should always be held responsible and it is never the target's fault. Despite knowing that, a woman can experience emotional and psychological consequences that can include depression, hopelessness, anxiety, feeling on edge, fear, and suicide. Such an attack can take its toll in eating and sleep disorders, self-harm (like cutting in secret), substance abuse, dissociation, and flashbacks, not to mention physical issues such as pregnancy and sexually transmitted infections. In addition to women having different issues at stake than men in an attack, you also have different approaches to combating an assault.

When you are able to trust your gut—that is, actively use your intuition—you are a step ahead. Your subconscious mind is wired for safety. It analyzes and processes your surroundings constantly, without your being aware of it, and will send out an alarm when it registers that things are not as they should be. This comes across as a sense of unease and can manifest itself in a variety of locations on the body. We have a whole myriad of expressions, such as "butterflies in your stomach" or a "tingling" on your skin, that reflect the different ways your brain communicates with you through physical sensations. By training yourself to pay attention, you can notice the messages your subconscious is broadcasting. The good news is that through practice, you can strengthen and develop your intuition. It is the most basic form of self-defense and one of the most powerful tools you have to stay out of harm's way.

Additionally, there are key practices and habits you can use to protect yourself. You may find that you are already doing some of these things naturally. For instance, the way you walk sends a message to the outside world, which includes would-be predators. They are on the lookout for a person who they believe will be easy to subdue and control. I will break down the steps you can take to project an image of assertiveness and energy when you are on the go that will make you an unappealing target. When you keep an eye out, your intuition will put you on guard. If you walk into a bar and the creepy guy in the back won't stop staring at you, you'll sense it via intuition. You'll be able to observe his movements during the course of the night, taking away his ability to catch you unawares.

By the time you finish reading this book, you will definitely be able to observe whether a person's demeanor is threatening and you will understand how to interpret behaviors that indicate you are being evaluated as a potential target. Plus, I'll give you ideas on what to say and how to act if you are accosted or surprised by a possible predator.

The stories included in this book are real. I have some form of involvement with all of them; either I personally participated in an investigation, or was told of an incident firsthand, or was asked to consult on a case by the media. I have combined these real-life experiences with commonsense tips and cop-tested strategies that will be new to many of you and, most important, not well known by potential predators.

Most of the time, all this knowledge will be enough to protect you. You will see the signs and remove yourself from a situation or know how to de-escalate an encounter. The use of force is something to be turned to as a last resort; in other words, when there are no other options left. In case you are selected by a predator, this book also includes a whole chapter on physical self-defense. You will know how to defend yourself and will send a message that you are not going to be easily intimidated and controlled.

The New Superpower for Women illuminates the greatest strength women have for preventing possible violent encounters: intuition. For years I've studied predator tactics and how to respond to them. As a certified defense tactics instructor, I have had, as students, members of the FBI, DEA, NYPD, Army Rangers, Navy SEALs, Delta Forces, London's Metropolitan Police, Ireland's Garda Síochána, and the Security for the State of Israel–Office of the Prime Minister. I've trained thousands of women in safety and self-defense through Defend University (www.DefendUniversity.com). In addition, I'm an instructor or black belt in multiple disciplines, including a third-degree black belt in Gracie Jiu-Jitsu under world-renowned instructor Phil Migliarese at Balance Studios,* and I hold the rank of associate instructor under world champion Shooto fighter and mixed martial arts trainer Erik Paulson.

* Under the lineage of Relson Gracie and Helio Gracie.

But at the end of the day, all my training and experience have led to one basic, essential lesson: women can use the intuition they are born with as their most effective defense tool. You just need to be trained to use it. And *The New Superpower for Women* is that training manual.

I'm an advocate and crusader for women's safety not just because of my experience in law enforcement, but because I myself was the victim of a sexual crime and understand the feelings of helplessness and frustration it engenders.

Always an avid athlete, in eighth grade I played linebacker on the local football team. During one game, while cross-body-blocking a player on the opposing team, I was thrown to the ground. Crack. That sounded like trouble for sure. An X-ray confirmed a broken back and I faced a week's hospital stay, replete with sponge baths—basically the whole nine yards—which was followed by six weeks confined to a bed.

Sitting in the hospital, before the days of iPhones and Kindles, and frankly, even before cable TV, was a serious drag for an active fourteen-year-old kid. These were also the days when Catholic priests were considered infallible and pillars of the community. So I was happy when there was a knock at the door and a priest walked in. Sure, I didn't know him, but it was, and remains, common for priests to visit hospitals and chat with patients who seek their counsel or spiritual comfort. After some small talk about my grades, the reason for my hospital stay, and my favorite subject at school, the priest asked if I wanted to make confession. Figuring it would be a nice gesture—after all, he had come to visit and made time go by faster—I said yes. What did I confess to? I don't remember anymore. Maybe to cursing. Maybe to being mad at my brother. Maybe I even promised to go to church more often.

Clear as day, I remember his response to my confession.

"Umm, Stephen, do you masturbate?"

Whoa. Now, I knew back then, as a fourteen-year-old, that this wasn't a question he was supposed to be asking. Thinking quickly, I thought I'd come up with the perfect response.

"I don't know what that is."

"Your back is broken, right, Stephen?" He put the Bible down on the nightstand. Raising the sheet, he pulled my pajama pants down and lowered my underwear.

Then he lifted my penis and said, "It's when you play with this."

Maybe it was the expression on my face. Or a sound in the hallway. I don't know why, but he abruptly walked out.

Soon after that my parents came, and I immediately told them what happened. The hospital was notified. The police were notified. My room was busy, as everyone crowded around the bed, asking questions. A doctor stood, taking notes.

One of the cops asked, "Hey, is he on any medication?"

His eyes met the doctor's and I saw an understanding pass between them.

"He has been on meds, though not anymore. . . ." The doctor turned to me: "Stephen, could this have been a dream?"

And that one question signaled to us that the doctor and police didn't believe me. My parents ended the interview right then and there. Although they hired a lawyer and a private investigator, there was no structure in place to report and follow up on the priest's behavior.

I consider myself lucky that the priest didn't go any further. Yet that brief encounter taught me what it's like to be on the receiving end of unwanted attention. The experience also shaped and guided my work in law enforcement. During my career on the police force, I concentrated on crimes against women. Those investigations led me to focus on preventing future assaults by using common sense and intuition and physical self-defense.

A key element in prevention is understanding how the perpetrator thinks: How does the perpetrator decide whom to target? What signals does he read that make someone seem vulnerable? What steps can women take to protect themselves? This knowledge, this awareness, which seems abstract and intangible, is very important—in fact, it can protect you from physical harm or even save your life.

My passion is educating and teaching women about the power of common sense, about their ability to prevent crimes against themselves and against their loved ones. I believe that up to one in four women will be the victim of sexual assault in their lifetime. While women of any age can be targeted, when we look at the statistics, we see that women between the ages of twelve and thirty-four are in the most vulnerable group. Educating young women in particular with firsthand knowledge about what a predator is looking for and about how to be a hard target, and providing them with solutions to situations that they may have to respond to under extreme pressure, protects them from future physical and emotional distress.

It is my mission, and that of all the instructors I train at Defend University, to foster confidence, awareness, and strength in women through education and preparation. You have the gift of intuition and can use it to protect and empower yourself, yet frequently that ability is set aside. Don't disregard this most valuable and powerful tool by not acting on your gut feeling.

1
INTUITION

·········

Susan, a young, attractive nurse, had recently moved to Seattle. She enjoyed walking her dog in the local park and would sometimes see a man with a pooch similar to hers.

Their paths soon crossed and he made a comment about the pets being twins. This brief encounter turned into regular conversations whenever they ran into each other. His name was John and she did notice that he seemed to be in the park often, almost every time she was there. What started as a mutual interest in their dogs quickly moved to flirting. While she enjoyed the attention, Susan began to pick up a strange vibe. Something was off, though she couldn't quite put her finger on it. Was it something he said, or a look he gave her, or was she just being silly? Since she was new to the area, she thought maybe she was being overly cautious, but still, she felt she should keep her distance.

One afternoon, John appeared seemingly out of nowhere and invited her out for drinks. She'd had a feeling this was coming and had even planned a response in advance. Although she was actually single, she said that she was seeing someone. A look of rage flashed briefly across his face. It scared her, but confirmed her gut feeling. He was visibly annoyed. This only added to her discomfort, yet she tried to keep the conversation light and friendly.

Although she had always looked forward to taking her dog out, Susan started changing directions if she saw John in the park before he saw her. One Saturday, as she was paying her dog walker, the walker mentioned that a guy with a small dog had stopped her a few times asking, "Is that Susan's dog?" When she responded yes, he'd asked probing questions, particularly about Susan's work hours and what time she'd be getting home. As the walker stated, "It was weird."

Susan managed to avoid John for about four weeks. One day she over-heard her coworkers talking about the grisly murder of a forty-year-old Seattle woman, who also happened to be a nurse. She'd been raped, mur-dered, and dismembered. Later that evening, to her horror, John's image was plastered all over the local news. He was responsible for the nurse's murder. Friends who knew him reported that he was hotheaded and un-restrained when he drank. He also had a history of violent felonies and had been arrested in five different states.

Susan was able to prevent a potentially dangerous situation by paying attention and trusting her intuition. Although John seemed nice initially, without her knowing why, he scared her. Her intuition was sending her signals to be aware, and she had followed them.

Your Intuition

A feeling in your gut. A subtle sense of foreboding. A hunch. Sometimes you'll have an immediate reaction to something without being able to articulate why. You may not have thought it through enough to come to a logical conclusion, yet you instantly know exactly how you feel or what you want. That is your intuition at work.

Intuition is knowing something without knowing why. It is how the subconscious mind communicates with the conscious mind, giving you the ability to make split-second decisions. You may have a strong feeling or a gut reaction, or you may have a sensation on your body, such as the hair on your arms standing up. Although you may not initially under-stand the underlying reason for your feelings, it is important that you pay attention to them.

Scientific and psychological studies have shown that intuition is an incredibly rapid cognitive process and one of the key elements in the decision-making process. While you are actively registering your surroundings with your eyes and ears, subconsciously your brain is working in the background, picking up additional information and details.

An astonishing 80 percent of your brain is dedicated to processing the subconscious, while only 20 percent is allotted to analytical and rational thought.* A sure sign that you should pay attention to what your intuition is trying to communicate to you.

Wired for Safety

The brain is specially wired to keep you safe as it processes information about people you are interacting with and your surroundings. First impressions are often based on a subconscious evaluation. Although you may not be aware of it, a person's clothing, the neatness of their hair, their posture, the expression on their face, even their jewelry sends a message that is most likely picked up and interpreted by your intuition.

In a business setting, you actively take steps to control the image you project. You may wear outfits that signal power or creativity; you choose a particular hairstyle and even learn to shake hands in a way that conveys assertiveness. In the work world, we are conscious of the nonverbal messages we send out and we pay attention to other people's signals because we expect to come into repeated contact with many of the same individuals and we want to influence their perception of us.

The same process of evaluation happens all day long, whenever you interact with people. Your brain sizes them up in a matter of seconds. Generally, in passing social interactions, you don't spend much time paying attention to what your subconscious is saying. If you did tune in, you might hear a little voice in your head sending feedback all the time.

Just as it is sensitive to people, your subconscious is also alert to the physical environment. An advertising agency may choose to decorate their offices with a modern, cutting-edge style to send the message that they are aware of trends and ahead of the curve. Although you may not be aware, your brain is registering and processing the details of your surroundings.

If you ever had the feeling you were being followed, it is possible that your subconscious picked up a sound that was out of the ordinary behind you, such as rapid footsteps, or your peripheral vision noticed something unusual. Maybe the person trailing you was hurrying because they were late for something, but an accelerated gait also matches the sound of someone

* Francis P. Cholle, *The Intuitive Compass* (San Francisco: Jossey-Bass, 2011).

attempting to catch up to you. It is noticed by your subconscious mind first, which sends an alert to your conscious brain. A fear signal appears so that you can react immediately to protect yourself from harm.

R-E-S-P-E-C-T Your Intuition

Traditionally, analytical thinking and logical reasoning are seen as the best way to come to a decision. You review the cold, hard facts, run through various decisions and their consequences, and then draw a logical conclusion. Going with your gut or having a hunch is not considered factual and is even viewed as a personal interpretation of events, biased by your preferences.

Yet I am here to tell you that utilizing your intuition is one of the best ways to protect yourself and your family. Most women who had been targeted in a crime sensed beforehand that something was not right. It may have shown itself in the form of the predator's body language, his posture, the way he walked, his glance, his demeanor, or any combination of many factors that, while difficult to pinpoint, caused the woman subtle discomfort.

Although the use of intuition is innate and humans have used it successfully for centuries to survive, there is frequently a moral evaluation attached to admitting that that's how a decision was made. You might be worried that it makes you seem overly emotional. It can be embarrassing to say that you followed your intuition rather than presenting your decision as the end result of a fact-finding mission. However, the only bad thing you can do with your intuition is to ignore it completely. In hindsight we often say to ourselves, "I should've listened to my intuition."

The New Superpower

Based on my experience, I believe that of the two sexes, women have the stronger sense of intuition. I have also observed that they are more likely to disregard or not follow their intuitive feelings than men are. They often realize after the fact that their gut reaction was spot on.

It is harder for women to respond in line with their intuition than it is for men because little girls are socialized to be nice, to be inclusive and take others' feelings into account. From the time they are children, females are expected to give hugs to relatives or family friends. You may have found Aunt Betty's second husband, "Uncle Rob," a total creep, but your gut instincts were overridden by social norms. As a female, you should be friendly and polite. As a result, many women ignore their intuition when they meet someone who makes them feel strange. Having intuitive feelings that something is not right about someone, even if it's someone you have just met and you have no concrete reason for feeling that way, is completely acceptable. You can be polite but keep your distance. And you are not required to hug anyone, ever.

You may also fear being viewed as judgmental when you feel something is wrong, rather than defining yourself as perceptive.

By developing your intuition and learning to listen and understand what it is conveying to you, you will have a powerful tool for staying safe. It will alert you when something is not right so you can put a distance between yourself and the situation or remove yourself completely.

My suggestion is to view the world, or at least the people you interact with, in a neutral light, until you get to know them. Listen to your gut feeling. You aren't unduly harsh or judgmental of people, but neither do you hand over your personal safety to someone you don't know.

Stranger Danger

When you think about potential predators and danger, you imagine an attack will come from a total stranger, from someone who knows nothing about you and means to harm you. But the truth is that most assaults and predatory attacks don't occur with total strangers but with individuals whom you may know in passing or have interacted with. In cases of rape or attempted rape, more than 70 percent of women know their attacker. This does not mean you know them well. It could be a fellow commuter you say hi to every morning when you pick up coffee, or even that nice guy who has a few mutual friends with you.

You should always have your guard up with a complete stranger, that is, someone you don't know at all, yet this habit should be expanded to many people with whom you have limited experience. Like if your roommate's new boyfriend shows up unannounced when she's not home. You don't know that he has bad intentions, but he is basically a stranger. If you know that she's not expected home anytime soon, have a preplanned response. You could say, "I have to leave in five minutes." If he tells you she is on her way home, double-check with her. Or, for example, you might think you know a student in your bio class. He always finds a spot next to you, and has started bringing you Diet Coke to help you make it through lectures. In that limited context, especially with other people around, yes, you do know him. However, if he asks you out to dinner, then under those circumstances you should use your intuition and common sense and similar precautions that you would with a stranger. He has not shown you how he behaves when people are not around. What if he suggests going to a party or bar after dinner, even volunteering to be a designated driver? You know that you would not get into a complete stranger's car, but without knowing him better, it is very similar. By the way, I would not recommend letting him drive you. Stay empowered by giving yourself choices and being able to leave whenever you want.

Instinct

While instinct is frequently used in the same context as intuition, it is a different process. An instinct or reflex is an inborn behavior that animals and humans engage in without thinking, such as a baby's hand grasping when you rub its palm or a wet dog shaking its fur to get rid of the water. In both cases the reactions are automatic, done without any thought. No one taught the infant to close its hand just as no one trained the dog to shake itself. Intuition, on the other hand, is a feeling caused by the accumulation of experiences and is part of an ongoing process of learning and responding to our surroundings.

When Intuition Knocks, Open the Door

While your intuition may sense something is off, it can be hard to interpret what exactly is wrong and whether you should respond. As in the following story, sometimes we believe our reasons for not listening to our intuition are stronger than for listening to it. Lisa and her mother enrolled in my self-defense course shortly before Lisa went off to college. Her mother hoped it would help her daughter when she moved out and it was a nice way for them to spend time together. I stayed in touch with Lisa throughout college, and in her sophomore year she visited during spring break.

She told me the story of how during that year she had gone on a date with a senior. He took her out to a nice dinner, where they shared a bottle of wine. She felt somewhat dizzy by the time the meal was over, yet he kept ordering more drinks for himself. After paying the check, he invited her to his parents' house to watch a movie. He mentioned that his parents were home, though they might be asleep.

Her gut reaction was to say no. She told me that she clearly knew that going to his house was a bad idea. But she was interested in him and didn't want their first time out on a date to end on a sour note. She was hoping they would start dating. So, going against everything that her intuition and her gut were telling her, she agreed to go home with him.

They got to his house and she followed him into the family room, which was in the basement. She would later learn that his parents' bedroom was on the third floor, at the opposite end of the house. Torn between feeling like she should go home and feelings of liking him, she settled on the couch to watch the movie. Dimming the lights, he drank half a beer. As the movie started, he gently placed his arm around her and they began kissing. Almost immediately, he pinned her to the couch and began groping her, attempting to unbutton her blouse.

"Get off of me," she said.

But he persisted and wouldn't let her go. "Get off of me," she repeated more loudly.

At that point Lisa resorted to a move we teach in class. She placed her hands under his chin, palms facing up, and forcefully pushed with an upward motion. We have a saying in class, "Where the head goes, the body will follow."

His head and his body were raised high enough for her to pull her legs up and kick him off her. Grabbing her belongings, she ran toward the door. He recovered enough to make it there before she did and he attacked again. She dropped

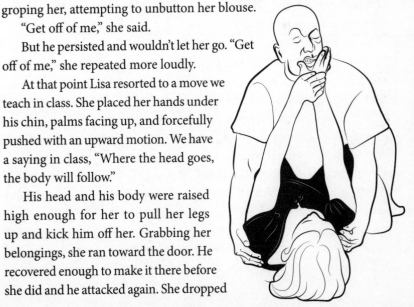

to the ground on her back, kicked him in the stomach and then the groin, and was finally able to run out.

Lisa had driven herself to his house in her own car and was able to leave of her own accord. Although she did see him during her remaining time at college, she chose not to speak with him and he never approached her to apologize. If she had gone to the police, he could have been charged with unlawful imprisonment, sexual abuse, and possibly attempted rape.

Sometimes your intuition will send you signals that you will choose to ignore. You may have other information that contradicts it, or you might not agree with your hunch, or you might not fully understand what your intuition is signaling to you. Lisa had had a gut feeling that going to his house was a bad idea, yet she liked him and hoped the date would lead to the beginning of a relationship. It is through habit and experience that you will become better able to interpret your subconscious brain's messages.

Practice, Practice, Practice

Although trusting your intuition is one of the most important steps you can take to keep safe, it's a scary one. You've never thought about it much and now you are expected to put your personal safety on the line by suddenly listening to an inner voice?

I understand that it might feel strange at first. But yes, harnessing the power of your subconscious and its ability to rapidly process information and compile it into a gut feeling can help you avoid dangerous situations.

The good news is that there are exercises you can do to bolster your intuition, to tune in to the voice in your head to get it to be clear and strong. Most of them entail stepping away from situations that require immediate action and response and instead creating an environment where the conscious mind can zone out, giving the subconscious a chance to process information and send you messages. Since you'll be doing something that doesn't have a sense of urgency, it will be easier to pick up on what the subconscious is saying. The messages you receive are your intuition in action. Following are ten exercises that will help you develop your intuition over time.

1. **Spend time in nature.** Spending time in nature gives you the chance to turn off outside distractions and pay attention to the signals or feelings your subconscious is sending you.

2. **Be creative.** When you're engrossed in creating, the subconscious runs in the background and makes connections and processes information.

3. **Learn from past events.** The more you can pinpoint receiving intuition signals and sensations during past experiences, the better you will be able to trust those feelings in the future. Remind yourself of moments you felt you knew something that later came true. Even if you didn't heed your own advice that time, acknowledging the role of your intuition will help strengthen it.

4. **Mix it up.** When you follow the same routine day in and day out, you stop paying attention to the messages your mind is sending. Change up your surroundings so you will force yourself to pay attention to signals from your subconscious mind.

5. **Listen to your gut.** See what kind of information you can gather from people before you talk to them. If you have a hunch, or gut feeling, about something or someone, pay attention to it. See if you're right.

6. **Meditate.** During meditation, the part of your brain that controls your movement and action is stilled, allowing the subconscious to process everything it has taken in and create feelings or sensations. Meditation can be as simple as sitting quietly in a room.

7. **Write down your dreams.** Both your dreams and intuition originate in the unconscious mind. By paying attention to your dreams, you will get in touch with your intuition. By writing down your dreams, you will be able to see patterns, or themes that are repeated, and you will gather a lot of information about what's in your mind.

8. **Work with your five conventional senses.** Exposure to different settings, situations, and people lets you put all your senses to work to aid you in understanding a new situation. Sight and sound are particularly key as your first line of defense. Consider writing down your observations in a journal.

9. **Breathe in, breathe out.** According to Dr. Belisa Vranich,* clinical psychologist and founder of the Breathing Class, your breath can give you cues as to how you feel unconsciously. Do you find yourself barely breathing around someone in particular? Make sure to take note *if* your body tenses up around someone and figure out why.

10. **Let it all out.** Intuition is a feeling and one of the ways to tap into it is to ask yourself, "How do I feel right now?" It is important to write down how you feel and to develop a refined emotional vocabulary.

The Second Brain: Your Gut

"Butterflies in your stomach," a "gut feeling"—we use these expressions to describe physical sensations related to intuition. Unknowingly, they depict the primordial brain-gut connection, which modern science is only now beginning to understand.

Scientists have learned that the brain and gastrointestinal system communicate through a long nerve known as the vagus nerve. The vagus is a cranial nerve, one of twelve nerves that arise in the brain and brain stem rather than in the spinal cord. The word *vagus* means "wanderer" in Latin (think: *va*gabond or *va*grant) and is appropriate for this nerve that weaves its way through your abdomen and influences many bodily functions, including heart rate and digestion. It is the primary channel of communication between the gut and the mind and continuously sends information back and forth between them. Interestingly, 80 to 90 percent of the nerve fibers in the vagus specifically transfer information about the state of your internal organs, or your viscera, to the brain.

Scientists have discovered so many neurons in the gut that they now refer to it as the "second brain." It does not seem capable of thought as we know it, but it is an integral part of the mind-body feedback loop. Visceral reactions and gut feelings are emotional responses originating in your stomach that are conveyed to your conscious mind via the vagus.

Messages ferried downward to the "second brain" include signals to

* Dr. Belisa Vranich is the author of *Breathe*. Learn more at www.thebreathingclass.com.

your organs that you are safe and that they can remain in rest-and-digest mode, or alarms indicating danger and triggering the fight-or-flight response in the body.

Communication between the gut and the brain is responsible for many things physical and emotional. This is a new field of study and research is being conducted around the globe on the connection between the two. Scientific studies support the importance of trusting our gut feelings.

Where Does Your Intuition Live?

Our language is full of expressions that capture the signs of intuition. Whenever you have one of the following sensations, it can be a signal that your intuition is communicating with you:

Dry throat
Lump in the throat
Hairs on the back of your neck standing up
Tingling on the back of your neck
Shivers up your spine
Chills down your spine
Feeling it in your bones
Butterflies in your stomach
A feeling in your gut
Tingle in your stomach
Tickle in your belly
Goose bumps

You may have had these sensations and ignored them, or maybe thought your body was reacting to the weather or to food you may have eaten. Next time you notice a physical reaction, however slight, take stock and see if there is a particular person or event that may be the cause.

TAKEAWAYS

- Our brains are wired to keep us safe through intuition.
- Intuition is a feeling resulting from the subconscious brain processing your surroundings.
- You can practice and improve your intuition.
- Your intuition never lies. Learning how to interpret it is key.

2
SEVEN SECONDS

●●●●●●●●●●

The corner of the parking garage was dimly lit, with overhead lights not casting much of a glow to see movement beyond a few yards. I looked around, scanning the ceiling for security cameras. The few that were present were aimed at the busy entrance. Perfect. There was a chill, too. Another distraction—the cold will often prompt women to focus on getting warm by buttoning up their coats. Also, the mall was full that day with busy holiday shoppers rushing to pick up last-minute gifts.

I slipped on a fake arm cast. To avoid leaving a trail, I made one myself, though predators can easily buy them in stores and online, even in bulk. In my faded jeans and dark-blue jacket, I look like a regular Joe. Plain, nondescript—a nice guy with an injured arm. Serial killer Ted Bundy* had the same look, and he used similar sympathy tricks to lure unsuspecting women into isolated areas. We all know how that ended for them.

I walked closer to the mall entrance, waiting between two parked cars just outside the security cameras' view. I pretended to fumble in my pockets as if I were looking for my keys, to further the illusion that I was not threatening.

But shoppers don't pay much attention to anything anyway, just enough to avoid the cars backing out of parking spaces or those circling the lot. Most of them walk with their heads down, rummaging in their purses for keys or phones. Or they have buds in their ears—chatting on a cell phone, listening to music. However, I paid very careful attention to whom and

---

* Ted Bundy, a serial killer and rapist, was one of the most notorious criminals of the late twentieth century. Connected to at least thirty-six murders, he was executed by electric chair in Florida in 1989. His charm and intelligence made him something of a celebrity during his trial, and his case inspired many novels and films about serial killers.

what I saw. Looking for the perfect target, I picked this spot so I could profile women walking to and from their cars.

First up—a mother and young child. The woman's blond hair was cut into a bob and her knee-length black coat was stylish. Her daughter's fluorescent-green jacket made her easy to spot in a crowd. Through the glass doors to the mall, I caught sight of them as they approached the garage. The woman came to a halt a few feet before the doors, set down the shopping bags, and got herself organized. Smart. She fished out keys from her purse and slipped them into her coat pocket. She had lots of bags but consolidated, putting the smaller ones inside the bigger ones. Her daughter had been skipping in circles the whole time, but came running over as her mother said something, reaching out with her hand. Hand in hand, they entered the parking lot.

The woman's eyes quickly scanned the cars and she spotted me immediately. Her look told me that she was no easy target. Cool, appraising, alert—I wouldn't be surprised if she'd noted the emergency exits in advance. There was no way I was approaching her and her daughter. I pretended to be looking for my car keys. Striding forcefully past, our eyes met. She was definitely going to keep tabs on me.

A short time later, a car searching for parking drove slowly past me. The driver, a female, glanced my way as she passed to an open spot nearby. She registered me and waited in her parked car to see what I was up to. After about a minute she got out, shoulders back, head held high, and walked at a quick pace toward the mall doors. She was not stopping for me.

Finally, I spotted the perfect mark for my intentions. A brunette in jeans and a long-sleeved burgundy sweatshirt approaching the lot from the mall exit. She carried only one bag yet rummaged in her purse and her pockets as if she didn't remember where her car keys were. I noticed the earbuds and thought she was likely listening to music, since her lips weren't moving in conversation. She then pulled something out from the bag and examined it as she walked toward me. Maybe double-checking that she got the right gift. A good sign—she was distracted, disorganized.

I decided the time was right to make my move. Treading softly, I approached her gradually, as if my arm really was broken and I wouldn't want to trip and fall by moving quickly. Predators do not want you to see them coming.

"Hey there."

Her head swiveled up. Surprised. She hadn't noticed me and I'd caught her off guard. She looked at me expectantly. "Hi."

"Mind giving me a hand? I need help." I gestured to the back corner of the parking lot. "I called security and am still waiting for them to show up. Broke my arm a few weeks ago."

Her eyes took in my cast and sling. To stop her from thinking too much and to keep her engaged—after all, I was trying to get her to an isolated corner of the garage—I kept up the light chatter and started taking measured steps, being sure to stay facing her, toward my car.

"They'll probably be here any minute," I said to make her comfortable.

I then walked backward slowly, while still talking to her. As is people's natural tendency, she followed me.

"Yeah, I just need to get this out." I opened the trunk and gestured toward a box inside, indicating she should lift it. She leaned forward and reached in for the box.

And just like that, within a minute, an unsuspecting woman was alone in an isolated area of a parking lot with a complete stranger, bending into the trunk of his car. In a matter of seconds, I could have thrown her in, duct-taped her mouth, bound her arms and legs, and driven off.

And it wasn't just her. Out of the eight women I picked that day, they all fell for my sympathy trick. In fact, in similar sociological trials, out of twenty-one women, I was able to get all twenty-one into situations that would have compromised their personal safety. This was a real-life social experiment, documented for NBC, that was done because of a spike in sexual assaults in New York City. Despite all my years on the force, and everything I'd experienced, it surprised even me how easy it was and that so many women didn't follow basic, common sense when dealing with a complete stranger.

Don't Give the Cloak of Invisibility to the Bad Guy

Criminals feel powerful when you are unaware of their presence. Being "invisible" gives them a distinct advantage: the element of surprise. Just as a surprise birthday party can render the recipient speechless, an unexpected attack has a similar effect. It can be so shocking that initially you may not be sure what is happening, let alone how to react. And a few seconds of freezing up or feeling paralyzed when you are with someone who has bad intentions is a very, very long time. A predator can grab your purse and run or pull you into an isolated location.

When you are oblivious to your surroundings, you are immediately transformed into the target that predators are looking for: someone who is unprepared and too stunned to react. You are what is known as a soft target. Easy to catch off guard, easy to startle, and easy to overpower.

Everyday distractions, especially the ones created by cell phones—such as texting, emailing, listening to music with earbuds—and things such as walking while reading a newspaper, daydreaming, or being lost in thought mean you will not be able to monitor your surroundings very well, facilitating unwanted criminal attention. It is almost as if you have given the cloak of invisibility to the bad guy. He notices you not noticing, and presses his advantage.

The women I approached in the garage were all distracted, whether they were listening to music on their devices, eating lunch on the go, talking on the phone, rummaging in their purses for their keys, or looking for their cars. Whatever they were doing, they were not aware of their environment. I literally loomed up on them. Purposefully, I didn't give them ample opportunity to pull themselves together and gather their thoughts and belongings. I immediately started talking at them, giving them no time to respond. Although their guts may have been sending them a signal to act otherwise, they couldn't process it or act upon it. They were not able to ask themselves whether I was sincere or if I really needed their help.

This tactic is similar to the one used by an aggressive salesperson and will be used by a predator, as it was by Ted Bundy, when he is trying to con you, or worse. Also, by wearing a cast and making a request for help, I made it even harder for them to say no. Playing off their desire to be kind and helpful, I found they were willing to give me the benefit of the doubt and put aside concerns for their personal safety in order to help me. And they did, every time.

Better to Be Rude than Sorry

Don't gamble with your personal safety by giving the benefit of the doubt to a stranger. It is wholly acceptable and good manners to state that you will help someone as best you can when you are in a place that is safe for you (such as making a phone call on their behalf after you are safely on your way in your car or inside your home with a door between you). If they are

SAFETY HACK

Clear corners with a wide angle. Whether you are walking around the corner of a building, a car, a fence, or a wall, put some space

between yourself and the corner when you turn. It will put distance between you and a would-be predator.

By standing next to tinted windows, the predator isn't seen by the woman until she rounds the corner and is surprised by his

presence. To an outside observer, he might simply look like a boyfriend waiting for his girlfriend. He's not doing anything suspicious to attract attention, such as crouching down or hiding.

Walking a few feet away from her car would create distance between her and the predator, making it harder for him to grab her and giving her more time to respond by either running or screaming as loud as possible.

in any way offended or act as if their feelings are hurt because you elected to do this, that is simply confirmation to always put your personal safety first.

The Seven-Second Rule: Don't Be the Chosen One

It can take a seasoned criminal less than seven seconds to size you up. To decide whether you would be easy to rob, assault, kidnap, or whatever else is on his mind. Count to seven now: One. Two. Three. Four. Five. Six. Seven.

In the time from when you started counting to when you finished, a predator would have given you the once-over and decided whether he was moving forward to attack or whether he would be looking at the person walking behind you as his potential target. Yup, that's how quick it is.

His two biggest fears are getting hurt and getting caught. This knowledge empowers you in case you are picked. Fight back and cause a scene. The predator wants to commit the perfect crime and, in those few seconds, he assesses whether he runs an increased risk of getting hurt or caught by choosing you.

In 1981, sociologists Betty Grayson and Morris I. Stein conducted a now-famous study* that cast new light on how assailants picked would-be targets. The researchers set up a video camera on a busy New York sidewalk and taped people walking by for three days, between 10 a.m. and noon. None of the pedestrians knew that they were being videotaped.

The tape was later shown to inmates in a large East Coast prison who were incarcerated for violent offenses (such as armed robbery, rape, and murder) against people unknown to them. The inmates were instructed to rate the pedestrians on a scale of one to ten, from "a very easy rip-off" to "would avoid it, too big a situation. Too heavy." This is the basis for the Seven-Second Rule.

Two striking facts stood out. First, there was a consensus about who would be easy to overpower and control. Every inmate chose exactly the same person. Second, and unexpectedly, the choices were not solely based on gender, race, or age, as you would expect. Older, petite females were not automatically singled out. What came as a surprise was that there were

---

* Betty Grayson and Morris I. Stein, "Attracting Assault: Victim's Nonverbal Cues," *Journal of Communications* 31 (Winter 1981): 68–75.

other criteria that influenced the decisions. The inmates read the pedestrians' nonverbal signals and used those to make their choices.

When questioned about why they picked certain people, many of the participants couldn't articulate what had triggered their preferences. It was a subconscious decision, based upon the traits a predator knows indicate a soft target. As the researchers probed further, they figured out that the inmates' selections were based on a mixture of nonverbal cues. Basic movements made by the pedestrians, such as the length of their stride, how they moved their feet, the way they shifted their body weight, and whether their arms swung while walking, came into play and were interpreted for signs of vulnerability.

While it may seem surprising that something as basic as walking conveys information about your mental and physical state, it is worth noting that experienced medical professionals can also tell a lot about your overall health and well-being through your stride, gait, pace, and posture. The extensive study of body language in fields such as psychology, neurobiology, sociology, communications, and anthropology, in addition to the interest shown by law enforcement, the FBI, and the CIA, attests to the power of these gestures. In this case, however, it was the criminals who were using the knowledge to select would-be targets.

The bravest thing you can do when you are not brave is to profess courage and act accordingly.
—Corra Harris

The speed and consensus of their assessments is instructive. You are evaluated in the blink of an eye for any sign that potentially marks you as uncertain or hesitant. While women and the elderly are frequently targeted for assault because of the perception that they are vulnerable, anyone who gives off an air of being weak can be pegged as easy to compromise.

On the flip side, since we know what movements and actions signal unease and uncertainty, you can take steps to protect yourself by changing your behavior, including modifying your walking patterns to project yourself as someone who would be difficult to subdue and who would likely cause a scene: in other words, a hard target. Even if you don't feel particularly strong or purposeful, you can teach yourself to walk in a way that makes you appear as if you are. With practice, you can get better at projecting the external image until finally you may even internalize it.

Take the Right Steps to Be a Hard Target

When you see a hero or heroine in a movie, ready to save the day, they stride forward, chin up, head held high, chest forward, and shoulders back, prepared to meet whatever challenges lie ahead. Take Katniss Everdeen, the young heroine from the book and movie series *The Hunger Games*, for example. Just by looking at the way she walks and holds herself, you can tell she is confident and determined. Even if you have the sound off or have never seen *The Hunger Games,* or barely understand the story, her self-assurance comes through by the way she moves. And yes, that is an actress in a role, but her walk conveys power and strength, and that is something you want to do, too. And yes, this behavior can be learned.

The following illustrations show different styles of walking and I go over some of the key body language signals that are markers of strength or weakness. The descriptions are exaggerated to help me get my point across. In reality, differences in stride or foot movement might be subtle, yet working together with other movements such as posture, alertness, and even level of energy, they convey an overall impression of how vulnerable you might be. You will be assessed by unfriendly eyes to see if you are weak, are easily intimidated, or suffer from an injury. When you know what the signs are, you can influence the signals that you send out to the world.

Ask a friend to record you walking across the room toward them to get an idea of how you look when you walk. I'd suggest doing it in several places, such as down the street, in the park, in the grocery store. Watch the videos, paying particular attention to your stride length, foot movement, arm swing, body weight shift, posture, and speed (when appropriate). Try experimenting with how you walk. Imagine that you are the heroine of a movie, ready to win the day, and record how you look when you walk with that in mind. Practice walking with purpose and confidence for a few days, get another recording of yourself, and compare the two. Is there a difference?

While you may not be able to consistently control the nonverbal signals you give off, the knowledge of what the criminal is looking for gives you an enormous advantage. You can try to incorporate that knowledge into your daily movements and influence how you are perceived.

Stride Right

WALK THIS WAY

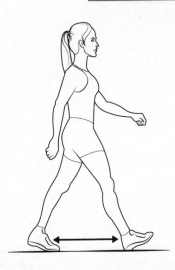

Stride length: *Take forceful, dynamic steps that convey assertiveness and confidence. The pedestrians in the study who were categorized as difficult to assault had a medium stride length when compared to their body height. When they walked, it looked effortless and natural.*

Foot movement: *Swing your feet gracefully forward. The pedestrians who were not selected swung their feet in a fluid motion.*

Arm swing: *When you walk naturally, your arms are slightly bent at the elbows, and you let them swing back and forth. It's natural for them to move to counterbalance your leg motion. When your left leg comes forward, the spine goes into a right rotation and the right arm moves forward. And then it repeats on the opposite side. The pedestrians who were not targeted walked with a swing to the arms.*

Body weight shift: *Walk smoothly, without jerking your body. Have an internal flow to your motion.*

Posture: *Your posture tells the world a lot about you and is an easy fix. Chin up, spine straight, and shoulders back, looking around, taking in your surroundings.*

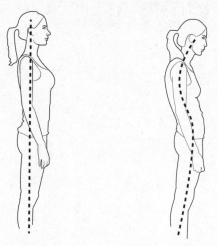

Speed: *Walk at the same pace as the foot traffic around you, or slightly faster. This way you won't draw much attention to yourself or, at most, you will give off the signal that you are more energetic or athletic than everyone else.*

DON'T WALK THIS WAY

Stride length: *The illustration above shows an abnormally long stride. Taking a long stride entails reaching out farther with your front foot, making you appear clumsy or ungainly. In a crowd, you will stand out as having a peculiar walk.*

Foot movement: *As mentioned, this type of stride makes you reach out awkwardly with your foot, almost as if you were making a small leap. All of the pedestrians selected as targets lifted their feet in a manner that was deemed odd.*

Arm swing: *When you take abnormally long steps, your arms will swing in a correspondingly uncoordinated fashion. They will fly up too high or appear to be flapping around your body. It can look comical and draw unwanted attention.*

Body weight shift: *With an extra-long stride, your arm swing may not be in sync with your legs, and you may look to be moving in a lumbering fashion as you shift from one leg to the other.*

Posture: *Be sure to indicate awareness of your surroundings. Don't give off the appearance of taking long steps, wildly swinging your arms, and being oblivious to who is around you.*

Speed: *Moving at an unnaturally rapid pace can make you stand out and appear nervous or fearful.*

DON'T WALK THIS WAY

Stride length: *The illustration above shows a shortened stride length, which can communicate caution or timidity. Almost like baby steps. Imagine a hiker with a twisted ankle, alone, trying to get back to camp before the sun sets. She may shorten her stride to avoid putting weight on the injured leg, sending off a signal of weakness and injury.*

Foot movement: *Every pedestrian who shuffled or dragged their feet was selected as a target. As were those who lifted their legs up and down and moved their feet in a vertical motion, like you may have done as a kid when you pretended to be marching, lifting your legs up with a bent knee and then down, rather than swinging them forward, feet first. It's similar to the kind of walk you might have when you wear new heels out for the first time and get blisters. Or you get those areas that are rubbed raw and are on their way to becoming blisters. Ouch. You start taking smaller steps, lifting your feet deliberately, even dragging or shuffling them to avoid the pain. This sends a subtle message that you are vulnerable.*

Arm swing: *A smaller stride length frequently corresponds with limited arm swinging. If your arms are pressed to your sides, immovable, you look clumsy and awkward. A limited swing is like waving a red flag that you are injured or scared. When you are nervous and afraid, you tense up, limiting your range of motion. Or you might be in pain, again sending the signal that you are fragile or delicate. In general, the shorter your stride length, the less you swing your arms and feet, making you appear to be walking with low energy and sending a signal that you are easier to attack.*

Body weight shift: *Most of the pedestrians selected by the inmates walked in a jerking fashion, their body weight shifting from side to side or up and down, reflecting an internal lack of synchrony.*

 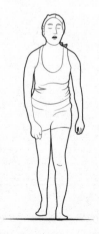

Posture: *A slumped or hunched posture, as above, sends out a message of fear and timidity, of being less likely to fight back. Similarly, walking with your*

gaze lowered or looking down suggests a lack of awareness, all of which make you an inviting target.

Speed: *Moving more slowly than the foot traffic around you sends a signal that you are possibly injured or weakened or simply distracted and not paying attention. Just as with zebras or gazelles on the wild plains, moving more slowly than the herd sends a signal to a predator that you are a soft target.*

The Split-Second Glance

As you go about your day, you want to be casually looking around, seeing what types of people are in your vicinity and registering your surrounding environment. This gives your intuition a chance to chime in and takes away any opportunities for a surprise assault.

I suggest giving people a split-second glance so that you have put them on notice that you know they are there. You are talking with your body and telling them, "I see you. If you're up to no good I know it, and I am not an easy target." When a predator knows that you have seen him, he may look for another target because the element of surprise is lost.

The split-second glance is exactly what it sounds like. You slightly turn your head toward the person you want to notify and flash a look in their direction. You don't even have to meet their eyes. It is almost like a brief nod. That's how subtle it is.

Many women I have spoken with believe that any glance can be interpreted as an invitation to interact. This one is different as it is extremely rapid and you do not necessarily meet the other person's eyes. You merely look in their direction, indicating your awareness.

Keep Your Head on the Level

After glancing over at someone, try not to instinctively incline your head. It is a natural reaction to look down afterward, but it can send the message that you are scared or timid. Train yourself to keep your chin level.

Remember to Be a STAAR

As you go about your day, remember to be a STAAR.

Stride: Take forceful, confident steps with a gait that is neither too short nor too long.

Tall: Shoulders back, chin up.

Arms: Let them bend naturally at the elbow and swing them as you walk.

Awareness: Take a look around as you walk, noticing people and things that might seem out of place.

Relax: Above all, stay calm, cool, and collected.

It may not be all that difficult to stand up straight, walk with determination, and be alert to your surroundings. The challenge is to keep it up for extended periods of time. When your phone pings, signaling that you have a new text or like, it is very easy to get distracted and forget to monitor the environment. The moment your chin drops and your awareness focuses on your screen, you turn into an easy target for anyone watching.

Yes, Trust Your Gut

As you look around, your subconscious brain will be picking up details and information and transferring that knowledge to your conscious mind as feelings or to locations on your body as physical sensations. In other words, your intuition will be actively giving you feedback. If it picks up something unusual, you will definitely get an alert. Train yourself to hear it no matter how softly it may initially caution you.

You have taken a critical step toward being a hard target by being cognizant of the way you walk and understanding that this is a key form of body language. It sends a message to everyone you meet, but most important, it is interpreted by predators and used to evaluate your vulnerability.

You've changed your stride, you are walking tall and determined and trying to notice people around you. Is there really much more you can do to maximize staying safe and still live your life without being scared and paranoid? The answer to that is yes, of course there is.

Police Academy Geometry

Law enforcement and other professions that focus on minimizing crime use the theory of the crime triangle to analyze and break down the main elements necessary for a crime to occur. When crime happens, it is not a random event. Usually it is a process that follows a certain sequence. If you understand the sequence of events, then you can take steps to reduce the risk of it happening to you.

According to the theory of the crime triangle, three things must exist in order to have a crime: a predator, a target, and an opportunity. Lacking any one of these, a crime will not occur. Law enforcement professionals focus on shortening the opportunity leg of the triangle, since that is where we have the most control. I am sharing this with you so that it is in the back of your mind and can guide your behavior.

Let's take a closer look.

OPPORTUNITY

Take the example of a woman walking through a quiet park on a sunny day. Suddenly a man runs by, grabbing her purse as he passes. Before she realizes what has happened, he sprints down the hill, through a gap in the hedge and onto the street, and presumably to a building or waiting car.

If we eliminate any of the legs of the triangle, we also eliminate the crime.

- If she had not been taking a walk in the park, the criminal/predator would have waited in vain. Eliminate the target and no crime occurs.

- Without the predator, the woman would have taken a relaxing walk through the park. No predator, no crime.

The first leg of the triangle is the predator, who needs desire, ability, and opportunity. It can be as simple as stealing a pocketbook or as complicated as robbing a bank, but someone out there has to be walking around with crime on his mind. The important thing to remember is that this is an element that we cannot control. No matter how many arrests are made, there will always be criminals. Individuals such as wives, close friends, relatives, siblings, peers, teachers, coaches, and other, similar people are outside factors that can influence the predator. In their absence, or if they have a weak role, crime is more likely to occur.

The next leg in the triangle is the target, which can be a person or a location. Anyone or anything can be targeted, depending on what a criminal is looking for. The police, security guards, and others whose job it is to protect people and property from crime can limit the likelihood of an attack being carried out. Other informal guards are parents, neighbors, friends, teachers, and peers, all of whom can look out for a target.

The last piece of the triangle is the opportunity. Once there is a criminal and a target, all that is necessary is an opportunity. A motivated criminal needs to be in the same place as, or have access to, an attractive target. And here you do have some influence and control.

Your goal is to reduce the opportunity leg of the triangle. You do this by paying attention to your intuition, by being aware of who is around you so you are not surprised, and by minimizing opportunities for criminals. For example, if you're out jogging and are tempted to take a shortcut through the isolated bushes home, don't.

Other ways to minimize criminal opportunities:

- Avoid secluded areas.

- Avoid poorly lit areas.

- Don't leave your pocketbook or cell phone unattended.

- Never leave your car running to do an errand, not even for a minute.

- Avoid allowing strangers into your home or living space.

- Don't be isolated with someone you don't know or trust.

- Always lock your windows and doors.

TAKEAWAYS

- In just seven seconds, a criminal will decide whether you make a good target. You will be physically assessed to see if you are weak or easily intimidated.

- By being aware of your surroundings you take away one of the predator's most important tools, the element of surprise.

- You can take steps to present yourself as a hard target by walking assertively: walk with purpose, head held high, shoulders back.

- Avoid creating opportunity for crime by avoiding environments that are conducive to crime.

3
AWARENESS

You Don't Choose the Day, the Day Chooses You

You have heard it time and time again: be alert, pay attention to your surroundings, know what's going on around you. Sure, if you find yourself walking down an empty street, late at night, your senses kick into overdrive. Entering a deserted ladies' room in the mall makes you uncomfortable enough to take a quick, sheepish glance under the stall doors to make sure no one is hiding in one of them. But other than that, you may wonder about the point of keeping your guard up on a busy street in the middle of the day. The chances of being mugged seem seriously low. Do you really need to be vigilant when you park the car at the local library or your doctor's office or the gym, when there are plenty of people coming and going?

The answer to these questions is yes. True, the likelihood of anything happening in broad daylight is minimal, but you want to develop a habit of noticing your surroundings at all times so that you are never surprised by an attack. You can't plan on when an attack could happen, but you can be aware most of the time so that you are always ready. You should be particularly alert and careful when you get to a new location, like when you leave a building or enter a bar. The situation is unfamiliar and needs to be evaluated.

Think of it as a low-level hum of mental activity. It's another way of saying have your guard up, but this is not about being hypervigilant or paranoid. It's closer to always looking both ways before crossing the street, a routine we learn as children that serves to keep us safe throughout our lives. Just as you would never walk across a street without checking for cars, you now are actively observant, particularly while on the go.

Situational Awareness

To be truly safe on a daily basis, you will need to develop the habit of situational awareness. You should know who is around you, what they are doing, and how that could affect you. Then you can take preemptive action to stay out of harm's way, whether this means just keeping an eye on someone or putting a distance between yourself and them or even leaving the premises. Later in this book I will walk you through situations that require more of a reaction than just avoidance.

Situational awareness is similar to what you do when you explore a new neighborhood. In that case, however, your curiosity is the force driving you to look around and get familiar with the surroundings. Imagine that you are in an unfamiliar place. Music blasts from an awning a few doors down and loud voices carry outside. You assume there's a bar, although you haven't actually seen it. Across the street you might spot a few restaurants where you can grab a bite to eat later. You're even clued in to their levels of formality by subconsciously registering how patrons are dressed. These types of observations are what you do when you are aware and actively noticing what's around you.

Situational awareness is a notch up from simply noticing things, since it involves trying to anticipate what will occur. It is a mindset that is routinely taught in the military and to law enforcement officers as a preventative tactic, particularly when they are on patrol. Not only do they scan their surroundings, but they also make assessments about what they see and their next move is made in anticipation of what they envision is going to happen. It is also used by workers in retail industries, particularly those that are prone to theft, such as drugstores, banks, and jewelry stores. They notice who comes in and, based on their level of experience in interacting with customers, they can assess their intentions.

One way of understanding the difference between basic awareness and situational awareness is to compare them to the different degrees of attention you practice while driving a car. With basic awareness, it is a given that you will be watching the stoplights, keeping an eye on traffic, and monitoring your speed. With situational awareness, you will also be doing those things plus looking ahead for possible mishaps. For example, if you are approaching an intersection and another car looks like it may not stop, you tap your brakes to slow your car in case the other one doesn't. You are preemptively anticipating any potential trouble and acting to prevent it.

With a little practice, you can develop a situational awareness mindset to the point that it becomes automatic. This habit is one of the reasons that in my more than thirty years in law enforcement, I have never been compromised. And once you use it a number of times, it will become second nature. Over time, your ability to detect behavior in other people that deviates from the norm and alerts you to monitor them will increase and be refined.

Situational Awareness and Crime

You may imagine that an attack starts with a gradual buildup toward violence, giving you time to pull back. A man approaches you and says something, you respond verbally. If he grabs you, you push him away. Next he might try to hit you, and you fight back. But the truth is that violence can happen suddenly and quickly. Police officers are used to seeing situations go from calm to out of control in an instant. Two minutes battling someone can feel like a lifetime. Even if you are able to dial 911 for help, when seconds matter, it can take law enforcement minutes to arrive. And that's why those precious seconds at the beginning of an encounter are so crucial and why you do not want to be taken unawares by a predator.

Using situational awareness increases your survivability in the event of an attack. The predator has lost the advantage of a surprise assault when you are alert to his presence and anticipating his next move. If he does decide to strike, you have made it harder for him and lessened his chances of success.

The First Twenty Seconds of an Attack

The first twenty seconds of an attack or assault are critical. During this brief window, you can still break away or discourage an attacker with forceful resistance. The longer you are in his close proximity, the higher your chances of being hurt. After twenty seconds the situation is more critical, but you should never give up fighting back. On many occasions, an attacker will give up if there is continued resistance.

The First Four Seconds of an Attack

On average, it takes half a second to four seconds, sometimes even longer, just to realize what is happening when you are subject to a blitz, or a surprise attack. You may be rushing to your car to get home from work or walking to meet a friend for dinner or going out for an early morning run. Suddenly a man appears at your side, or he comes up behind you. He may be trying to ambush you, either for robbery, sexual assault, or both. Four seconds may not sound long at all, but during that brief period you can be dragged into a car to be taken somewhere else (known in law enforcement as the "secondary location") or pulled behind a dumpster or into a building. If sexual assault is the intent at that moment, then it is likely that you will be on the ground within five seconds. You likely won't know what is going on and you probably won't know how to react. You may have an adrenaline surge and start struggling and trying to get out of a predator's grasp, but that surge will be brief. After that, you are spent.

Situational Awareness and Your Senses

Developing your situational awareness entails using all of your senses to monitor your environment. You might think you already do this automatically. You hear cars and sirens, you see people walking in front of you, you smell the aroma of coffee when you walk by a café. But if someone asks you what the server who brought you lunch was wearing, you may draw a blank. And that's what happens when you go throughout your day without actually registering what the brain is processing.

To bolster your situational awareness, you need to be genuinely mindful and cognizant. You need to consciously think about actively utilizing all your senses and not zoning out because everything seems normal and there is no obvious sign of danger.

Believe Your Ears

Although you gather most of your information using your eyes, your hearing is acutely tuned in to your surroundings. The brain processes sound much faster than it does sight, anywhere from twenty to one hundred times faster. As a result, auditory feedback creates an almost instantaneous, emotional reaction. Your ears lay the groundwork in shaping your interpretation of your surroundings.

In the distant past, rapid processing of noise gave us a survival advantage. At night, there were no streetlights, not even candles to help us see, and we relied largely on our auditory perceptions. Similarly, in jungles and forests, where we were surrounded by thick foliage and impenetrable vegetation, our sight was not very helpful. But our ears could still gather information and provide us with feedback as to who or what was in our vicinity.

You hear sounds all day, but you don't always pay attention to them. Only after there's a change in what you expect to be normal for a given place or location will you really start listening. With situational awareness, you pay more attention to things that you might normally ignore, such as the sound of shouts or quick footsteps behind you. By trusting your gut reaction to what you hear, you will be more adept at identifying threats.

The Eyes Have It

Sight is our most dominant and keenest sense. You recognize faces and process facial expressions, you react to quick movements, you see colors and have depth perception. However, while you rely on sight for most of the input to your brain, it may not always be as solid and factual as you would like to believe.

Your brain ignores images that don't seem important to what you are doing. Detectives and other members of the law enforcement community know that eyewitness accounts of crimes have proven to be unreliable over time. An eyewitness is not always enough to prove a crime, nor is one accepted as one hundred percent reliable. Corroborating evidence may be needed as well.

You can try to recall what you saw, but if it did not seem important at the time, your mind automatically would not expend energy by processing it. It's this brushing off of information that can be your downfall.

Through practice, you can train yourself to register more about your surroundings. You can notice unusual behavior, pay attention to facial expressions, be aware of exits in a building, or open windows.

Smell

While we think of smell as a sense that is highly developed in other animals, it is similar to sound in that it connects directly to the brain and triggers an emotional reaction. A bakery gets our attention when the aroma of bread wafts through the air, not just because of an artful window display. A particular scent can take you back to your childhood in a second or instantly cause your mouth to water.

Nowadays we assume that our sense of smell is not very strong, yet Native Americans and other hunters were often able to track animals not only by their prints and broken branches, but also by their scent. It is a skill that can be developed over time and with practice, though it's one we don't need very frequently. There are even some people who can pick up on fear or stress in other humans through smell. For purposes of situational awareness, a strong odor of alcohol may warn you about an altered mood or change in behavior. Or you may smell fire, or cigarette smoke.

Touch and Taste

These senses will not come into much use as you strive to be situationally aware. You may sense a taste in your mouth if you are near a fire or close to someone who is smoking. And touch will be useful if you are in the dark, such as a stairwell with a broken light, and are feeling about around you.

Keep Your Head on a Swivel

In law enforcement, we have a saying: Head on a swivel and watch your six. What this means: Keep an eye on your surroundings, from all sides. Know who or what is on your left, your right, and behind you.

The term comes from the image of a clock. Think of looking straight ahead as looking at noon. When you turn your head to the left, most of us look naturally between nine and ten o'clock. Using peripheral vision, a glance farther left requires a subtle twist, to about seven and eight o'clock. Similarly, when we look to the right, our gaze typically rests between three and four o'clock. A glance farther right using our peripheral vision brings us between four and five o'clock.

Watch Your Six

A cool way of saying: Watch your back.

When you are in an active state of scanning, periodically peek over your shoulder, nonchalantly, not projecting any worry or concern. And don't be afraid of putting someone on notice with a split-second glance that you are aware of their presence.

The phrase "Watch your six" goes back to the image of a clock. Think of noon as straight ahead and six o'clock as directly behind you.

Scanning Exercise

Usually you will be aware of who is in front of you, between 11 a.m. and 1 p.m. The situational awareness mindset means increasing your awareness to know who is on either side of you and behind you, so that you have as much information about your surroundings as possible.

Imagine that the room you are in is a clock. Stand at the center of the room and put your arms out at your sides.

Look straight ahead—that is twelve o'clock.

Look to the right—that is three o'clock.

Look to the left—that is nine o'clock.

To watch your six, or look behind you, shift your shoulders and turn your head a little farther to the left or the right. Think of it like a shoulder shimmy. You don't want to necessarily turn your whole body around, since that might send a message that you are afraid or worried.

Keep Your Eyes on the Prize

From prehistoric times, our intuition, our sight, and our hearing have kept us safe and those senses still work to protect us now. It sounds so simple and basic. And yes, in theory it is easy. But these days it is even easier to be distracted and to stop paying attention. Frequently you turn off the awareness switch much too quickly, without even realizing it.

High on the list of distractions is the use of smartphones in public, with their endless streams of texts and emails. Hunched forward, head angled down, you barely engage with the real world. The latest text or Instagram post or tweet occupy all your attention. You've given away your visual sense.

Heading toward your car, you are absorbed by a phone call. Or music blasts from your earbuds, preventing you from hearing what is going on behind you as you approach the ATM, throwing away your auditory sense and some, if not all, of your awareness.

You take the same route home every night and over time it feels safe and familiar, so you stop paying attention. You get lost in thought as you walk toward your apartment, planning a night out with friends or mulling over a recent conversation. And again, you don't notice much because you feel safe.

Carrying bags in a disorganized fashion, so that some are falling and you constantly have to adjust them, or rummaging in your purse for your keys is a similar distraction.

Do a mental review before you head out to make sure you have everything you need and that you know where everything is. Have car keys easily accessible, know where your bus pass is, organize your bags so they are easy to carry. If you must text or talk, step to the side, preferably with your back to a wall. Make it quick, and head on a swivel.

Establishing a Baseline

Every environment, and every person, has a baseline of what is "normal" noise and behavior for a given event or location. Baselines will vary. At the beach, the baseline might include children shouting and adults calling loudly to overcome the noise of the waves. At a baseball game, people scream, cheer for their team, wave their arms, jump up and down, and high-five one another. Strolling through a park, the baseline might entail hushed background noise, the sounds of children playing and birds singing. In New York City, fire truck and ambulance sirens are part of the sounds of the city, whereas in the suburbs nonstop sirens might mean that someone is in need of help or something serious has happened.

Wherever you go, you should mentally register what the baseline should be so that you are alert to anomalies, or aberrations, from the expected. Any type of behavior that does not fit in and deviates from the landscape or crowd should be noted. For example, overtly aggressive conduct or speech always deserves your notice and scrutiny because it is usually not appropriate. Other things that might draw your attention include leering, someone talking to themselves in an overly animated way, or a person who is unduly watchful and nervous, their eyes rapidly darting back and forth. This could be a predator looking for an opportunity to commit a crime.

In Nice, France, during the 2016 Bastille Day celebration, a terrorist drove a large box truck into a pedestrian-only area and through the crowd, injuring and killing a large number of people. We would expect the baseline in a public celebration to include the din of the crowd, the bang of fireworks, and the sounds of revelry.

What deviated from the baseline was the revving of a truck engine, the screams, the sight of a wave of people moving away from the truck's path and, eventually, the sound of gunfire. A similar attack was replicated in December 2016 at a Christmas market in Berlin. A stolen truck was again driven through a crowded public space.

In the Boston Marathon bombing, the bombers were noticed in surveillance footage because they looked calm while everyone else around them was running in panic. They knew in advance that the explosion was going to happen and weren't surprised.

Establishing a baseline for your environment is a start to enhancing your awareness ability. During a walk through a quiet park, you may suddenly hear angry yelling off in the distance. You don't need to know exactly what the people are saying to realize that something is not right and you should probably remove yourself from the area, and/or call for help.

Exercises to Develop Situational Awareness

Below are a few simple exercises you can do to improve your situational awareness abilities. Practicing these drills when you are relaxed and not under pressure will help develop this mindset so it kicks in automatically, even if you feel stressed or threatened. Most important, you will consciously recognize that something is wrong, so you can be proactive and immediately take steps so that you are not a target of criminal behavior.

Using situational awareness means trusting your gut feeling. The subconscious notices subtle signs of danger that are not processed as quickly by the conscious mind. The hair on your neck standing up, a chill running down your spine, knowing something without knowing why—all these are possible indicators that you have picked up on a person with ill intent, even though consciously you will not know what is setting off these triggers. Even without practicing situational awareness, you may still intuitively understand that certain behaviors or situations are potentially threatening. Maybe you will have a funny feeling without being able to explain why. When you do register someone or something unusual, try to leave, put distance between yourself and the person, or make your way toward other people.

To increase your situational awareness, do the following on a regular basis:

- When you enter a building, look around and identify all the exits.
- After visiting a store or a restaurant, try to recall what the salesclerk or waiter was wearing.
- Count the number of people in a restaurant, or on the bus or subway or train car.
- When you are in a parking lot, look for—and count—the number of cars with people in them, regardless of whether you are

walking to the store, returning to your car, or simply driving through.

- Try to work up a profile on a particular person. What do they do for a living? Are they well-to-do? Are they working class? Are they happy? Or sad? How do they interact with other members of their group?

- And my favorite: People-watch when you are in a restaurant. Sit with your back against the wall and study the different people and their interactions.

Stop. Before you read on, study the picture above for sixty seconds. Then read the following questions and see if you can answer them without returning to the image:

- How many people total were involved in this accident?

- How many males and how many females?

- What objects were lying on the ground?

- What injury did the man on the ground seem to be suffering from?

- What was the license plate number of one of the cars?

How did you do on this test?

Stop, Look, and Listen

When you stop, look, and listen, you let your senses work together to provide you with information about what is happening in your environment. You gather feedback so you can make an assessment on how to proceed. This type of practice is valuable to avoid not just the criminal element, but also other types of hazards or dangers.

The police use it every single time they are called to a situation. For example, a police officer may be dispatched on a domestic violence call. Upon arriving at the scene, he'll park his car a short distance from the actual address. This gives him a tactical advantage in approaching what might be a volatile situation. Once he exits the car, he will stop, look, and listen before he proceeds to the front door. Before he knocks or enters, he will again stop, look, and listen. Is there silence? Is there normal tone and discussion? Is it a loud and aggressive verbal exchange? Is there screaming? Based on what we hear, we create a visual of what is going on in the house.

Doing this gives the officer a better understanding about what situation he will encounter on the other side of the door. It tells him if he needs to get into the house because the situation has turned violent quickly and whether he needs to call for backup.

SAFETY HACK

Keep a mental note to immediately leave an area and seek safety when there is an obvious abnormality or change in behavior. For example, screams in a mall or movie theater can indicate an active shooter. If you hear what sounds like fireworks in a public place, go in the opposite direction. Don't let curiosity lead you into the fire. Use your auditory and visual senses to guide you without confirming who or what it is.

Alert: Location Change

While you strive to automatically scan most of the time, there are times when it is especially important. The rule of thumb is to pay extra attention when you are changing locations or are in a situation with unfamiliar people. The reason is that there are new factors in the environment and they need to be assessed and evaluated. Times to be particularly aware:

Whenever you are entering or exiting a building:

- When entering: Make a mental note—is there a doorman or security guard? Where are the emergency exits? Take a look at the lighting: Is it well lit, are there security cameras?
- When exiting: Look left, look right, who is outside? Check if there are people hanging about or loitering nearby. They could be predators looking for a soft target.

When you go to a bar or to a big party, especially a fraternity party or a house party where you don't know many people:

- Look around and take note of who is watching you, especially when you enter. This is when predators frequently spot their targets.
- Consider the baseline: Is it loud and rowdy even though it is early in the evening?
- Consider the behavior of other people: Is there a keg? Is there a common punch bowl? Are people drinking shots? Is there a bartender?
- Know where the exits are.

When you drive into a parking lot:

- Don't hang out in your car. Sitting inside limits your visual and auditory senses and curtails your ability to utilize situational awareness.
- See if there are any people loitering about; it's always better for you to spot them before they spot you.
- Before exiting your locked car, carefully check your surroundings, even if you are in your own driveway.
- Avoid parking in isolated areas. Try to park under a lamppost and close to the entrance.

SAFETY HACK

I suggest backing into a parking space whenever possible or driving into a space facing outward. Apart from the fact that both minor and very serious accidents occur when trying to back out, backing out can be difficult and your situational awareness diminishes during this process.

Other public places:

- Be very careful at the ATM, day or night. Attackers will stand fifty or more feet away and watch to see who is a soft target. You may never see them coming.

- When entering a mall or movie theater, take a few seconds to locate the exits. It is those seconds that could save you in a time of crisis.

In the Zone: Fight-Flight-Freeze

As you are scanning and processing your surroundings—in other words, employing your situational awareness—your level of attention will go up and down in response to what is happening around you. Over time, you'll effortlessly increase your focus at certain times and you'll know instinctually when to decrease it.

While you will be doing this automatically and without much thought, your mental processes and heart rate change according to the level of stress caused by your surroundings. Stress responses are so well established that a color code, known as the Cooper Color Code, was created by Lieutenant Colonel Jeff Cooper of the U.S. Marine Corps for combat scenarios. I have modified this version, tailoring it for women in noncombat scenarios, providing expanded information on how heart rates affect motor skills (important for self-defense) and decision-making abilities.

When we are scared, our flight-or-fight response kicks in to put the body and the mind into a condition that will help us survive an actual or perceived threat. Fear becomes the dominant emotion in the flight-or-fight response, bypassing the rational mind and resulting in irrational thought processes. When it perceives a threat, the brain initiates the release of a surge of chemicals into the body, mostly consisting of adrenaline.

Several things happen during this surge. First, blood flow to large muscle groups, such as the legs and arms, increases, since these muscles are most needed to escape or to fight. Your heart and breathing rates will intensify in order to increase oxygen intake to fuel those muscles. The body also pulls blood away from the extremities, such as fingers and toes, and into the torso. This keeps blood near vital organs in case of emergency and protects the smaller limbs and digits from losing too much blood in case of injury.

The increase in adrenaline combined with the loss of blood flow to the extremities can cause mild to excessive shaking of the hands (and feet) and the loss of fine motor skills. Your performance drops dramatically, making it difficult to perform even simple tasks, such as dialing a phone (like 911) or opening a car door with your keys (and getting in, to safety). Interestingly, exercise-induced heart rate increases do not have the same effects on motor skill deterioration as do chemically induced heart rate increases. The best ways to manage the effects of an adrenaline surge is to have a plan for what you will do under stressful circumstances. By preparing mentally in advance, you will automatically take those steps, without giving them much thought. Later in this book I discuss making a plan, or blueprint, and how it helps to control the adrenal response.

The following heart rate numbers are an approximate range only. Heart rates will vary depending on your level of fitness, life experience, and readiness.

The color codes are a guide to your level of alertness. At first, you will consciously strive to have the appropriate levels of alertness, depending on your situation. Over time, it will evolve to something you do automatically. Many ER nurses, paramedics, and police develop the ability to scan and evaluate a situation or individual and make a quick judgment as to whether it can be threatening to them. While initially they may have done it consciously, with experience it becomes an act of unconscious decision making.

The White Zone

When you are in the white zone, you are relaxed and unaware of what is going on around you. It is comparable to sitting in the security of your own home, in comfortable surroundings, watching television. And ideally, you should only be in this state in a secure location with the doors locked.

At this level, your normal resting heart rate is 60 to 80 beats per minute and all tasks and skills seem easy. Once you leave the safety of your home, you need to switch into the yellow zone.

The Yellow Zone

Whenever you are on the go, you should be in the yellow zone. You're almost as relaxed as in the white zone, but you are now scanning to see who and what are around you. It does not mean that you are scared or have an irrational fear of other people or places. You are simply alert and paying attention. You may observe an argument between two people over a parking spot. Or you may notice a group of unruly kids, milling about, possibly looking for trouble. Due to their proximity, these are events that could affect you. But since you are now difficult to surprise, you are not a soft target.

Generally, when you are out and about, you will spend long periods in the yellow zone. When something catches your attention, you focus on it. Anything or anyone that is unusual or out of place or out of context should be assessed.

In the yellow zone, your heart rate will remain unchanged from the white zone. From walking and moving it may be slightly elevated, but not as a result of an adrenaline surge. No motor skills are affected, though your senses are heightened as you are in an alert state.

The Orange Zone

In the orange zone, you will have noticed something or someone that may or may not be a threat. Until you determine what it is, you focus on it to make sure no threat exists. The difference between yellow and orange is that there is a specific target for your attention. By homing in on something concrete, you cause the escalation in alert status.

When you shift upward to orange, you are now concentrating on the person who caught your eye, and you continue to monitor what is around you as well. You don't want to be caught unawares, in case he has accomplices. You start to watch him and assess his intentions. Once you figure out he's not a threat, you can relax and go back into the yellow zone.

In the orange zone, you can expect your heart rate to fluctuate between 80 and 115 beats per minute. If you notice two men arguing and you are able to leave the area, your heart rate may have initially gone up but will begin to go back down. If you realize you are being followed, your heart rate will start increasing as adrenaline surges through your system in the fear response. As your heart rate approaches 115, you are entering the area where fine motor skills start to deteriorate.

The Red Zone

When you are in the red zone, you are likely experiencing a criminal assault or attack. You may have tunnel vision, concentrating on the predator in front of you, and not be able to defend against threats from other sides, for example if he has friends or accomplices.

Some people freeze. Some run. And some are trained and try to use the skills they have learned. Similarly, if you were in the wilderness and saw a grizzly bear, you would freeze first, in hopes it wouldn't see you. Next you would take flight and try to outrun it and finally, as a last resort, you might fight.

In the red zone, your heart rate will be between 115 and 145 beats per minute. On the lower end of this elevated rate, fine motor skills start to deteriorate. These are skills that usually require high levels of hand-eye co-ordination and involve meticulous movements using small muscle groups, such as handling keys, dialing phones, writing, and grabbing and picking up small objects. Complex motor skills, defined as actions that link three or more components in a sequence that requires timing and coordination, also deteriorate. Many martial arts techniques are complex motor skills. They may work in a low-stress environment, such as during training in a dojo, but fail in a high-stress situation such as an attack. You can, however, still use gross motor skills to defend yourself.

The Green Zone

In the green zone, you are under attack and probably fighting back. You have lost the ability to utilize fine motor skills (used for dialing 911), and your complex motor skills (necessary for martial arts) have deteriorated. However, at a heart rate of 145 to 175 beats per minute, your gross motor skills, useful in defending yourself, can actually improve. Gross motor skills are simple, large muscle group movements, including running, kneeing, elbowing, slapping, punching, pushing, and kicking from the ground. We call it the green zone, as in "green means go," because at a heart rate of 155 these skills thrive.

The techniques we teach at Defend University's women's self-defense classes involve the gross motor skills that work well in this zone. Many of them will be covered in Chapter 7.

The Black Zone

This is also known as the Frozen Zone, where you could be so overcome by fear that you freeze up and are unable to respond or react. It is a catastrophic breakdown of mental and physical performance. You are not prepared for a violent encounter mentally or through self-defense training. Your heart is racing at over 175 beats per minute and you are overwhelmed with stress. Both your mind and body shut down, immobilized with panic. You will be unable to make any decisions, such as whether to run or defend yourself, or even how to fight back. Visually, you will lose depth perception, experience tunnel vision, and most likely undergo auditory exclusion. This means that you will have trouble seeing your attacker, and possibly you will not register what people are saying to you. This can result in great harm to you.

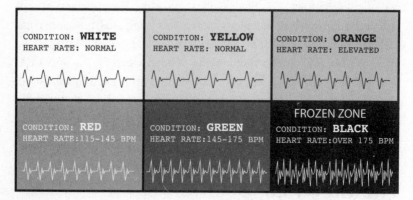

Pre-indicators

Awareness and intuition can play a key role in helping a woman combat being targeted for an attack. The unconscious aspect of the human mind protects you by picking up on cues that may indicate a pending attack. Frequently, there are nonverbal signals, known as pre-indicators, communicated by a predator that suggest ill intent.

A predator's behavior changes as he moves closer to selecting a possible target and attacking. These pre-indicators are visible in his body language and will give you a clue as to what he wants. You can pick up on them and realize that something is amiss, even if you aren't exactly aware of what it is. Following are some pre-indicators to watch for.

Target Selection

Predators look for a manageable target, usually a woman who they believe will be compliant and give the least resistance. A predator does not want to attack a woman who he thinks will scream and fight back and cause a scene. Although assaults against women are portrayed as being totally random, carried out by strangers out of the blue, in the majority of cases the predator and target have some knowledge of each other.

Frequently a predator will have evaluated a woman's level of compliance before attacking her. This is often referred to as the predator's "interview." He will attempt to engage in conversation by asking for directions, making a comment about the weather, or inquiring about the time. It is usually someone who makes you uneasy or looms up, surprising you. He may be checking to see how close he can get to you. It may feel out of place and your intuition may be kicking in, giving you the sense that something is not right. Don't stop to answer him, and keep moving. He may try to block your path. If he does, step around him. Do not engage with him.

Scanning

Scanning is when someone pays heightened awareness to the surrounding area. A predator might be looking for a target, formulating an escape route, or checking out potential witnesses. He can be observed scanning when he moves his head from side to side while his eyes appear to be searching. If you are his target, he may not even look at you. It might not be obvious what he's looking for, but when you are in the vicinity of someone who is scanning, you need to be on alert. Situational awareness will help you in advance by answering these questions:

- Are you in an isolated area?

- Can you get to people for help?

- Can you make noise to get attention?

- Have you checked out the surroundings and know where exits or escape routes are?

Target Glance

A predatory or target glance is easy to pick up if you are looking. A predator may be looking at your purse, wallet, ring, or anything of value that has caught his attention. He may also be checking if you are armed. He may even glance at your valuables and then lift his head looking around for an escape route. If his intent is to assault you and he is in proximity, he may look at your face, your nose, or your jaw and then position himself close to you so that you will be easy to strike. If an assault is imminent, he may adjust his feet and blade his body so he can launch an effective attack. Try to remove yourself from the situation, put distance between yourself and a potential predator, or attract attention and get other people involved.

Recognition of Emotions

Situational awareness will guide you in recognizing facial expressions and understanding how people are feeling. A predator will not give you a verbal warning of his intentions, but often clues to his intentions will flicker across his face. And if you are alert and paying attention, you are more likely to spot them. These are called macro-expressions and all people can see them. Facial expressions are hard to control. By recognizing these emotions, you can react quickly to help ensure your safety in case the expressions indicate danger.

In studies of more than fifteen thousand people over the past two decades by psychologists Paul Ekman and Maureen O'Sullivan, only fifty individuals were identified who could spot deception with exceptional accuracy. These individuals, referred to as "truth wizards," are able to register micro-expressions, expressions that flash across a person's face in half a second or even in a quarter of a second. Micro-expressions are hidden emotions, ones that a person doesn't want you to see but that leak out.

However, according to Renee Ellory,* one of the truth wizards, Ekman established seven universal expressions for emotion that are expressed by every human on the planet. We make these seven expressions exactly the same way, using the same muscles, regardless of where we were born, what language we speak, or where we live. These emotions are: happiness, surprise, sadness, fear, contempt, disgust, and anger.

When a person makes each of these emotional expressions, they move specific muscles on the face, and you can learn to recognize these expressions by noting distinct features for each emotion. Understanding these expressions will give you the confidence you need to quickly assess someone, know how they are feeling, and act to protect yourself if necessary.

You can practice observing people and seeing which emotions appear on their faces and when. Another good place to watch for facial expressions is on television, whether it is reality television or sportscasts and news shows. Keep an eye out for their facial expressions.

For purposes of safety, the most important emotions for you to be able to identify are disgust, anger, and contempt. During the presence of these emotions, a person is much more likely to lash out physically. If you register them on someone's face, alarm bells should go off and you should move yourself to a distance.

* Renee Ellory has trained thousands of law enforcement professionals across the country, consults with law enforcement on challenging cases, and is considered to be an emotionally intelligent genius by scientists. Learn more at www.eyesforlies.com.

HAPPINESS

A real smile always includes:

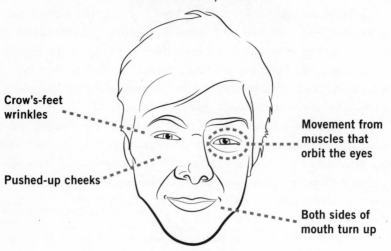

Crow's-feet wrinkles

Movement from muscles that orbit the eyes

Pushed-up cheeks

Both sides of mouth turn up

SURPRISE

Lasts for only one second.

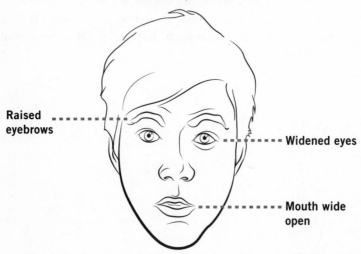

Raised eyebrows

Widened eyes

Mouth wide open

SADNESS

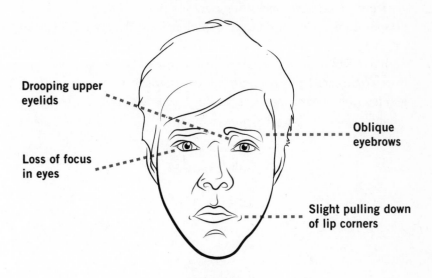

Drooping upper eyelids

Loss of focus in eyes

Oblique eyebrows

Slight pulling down of lip corners

FEAR

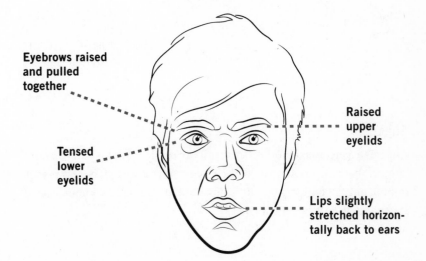

Eyebrows raised and pulled together

Tensed lower eyelids

Raised upper eyelids

Lips slightly stretched horizontally back to ears

Disgust

Disgust is a basic, primordial emotion showing repulsion. Initially it alerted us to horrible smells that were indicators of death, disease, or poison. Think of the rancid smell of decomposing flesh or the stench of rotten eggs.

In modern times, a predator may show disgust on his face because he hates women, and hence is more inclined to attack them. Or a street person may feel disgust when looking at wealthy people who flaunt their wealth, reminding him of his limited financial straits.

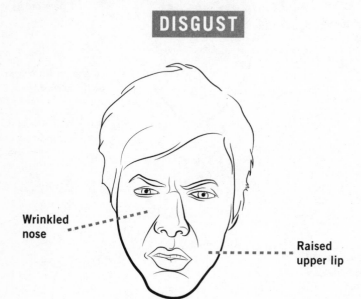

DISGUST

Wrinkled nose

Raised upper lip

Anger

Anger is a dangerous emotion because it can escalate quickly and you don't know if that person can control their anger. If you see a homeless person ranting angrily on the street, it is best to step away. The combination of anger and disgust can equal rage.

ANGER

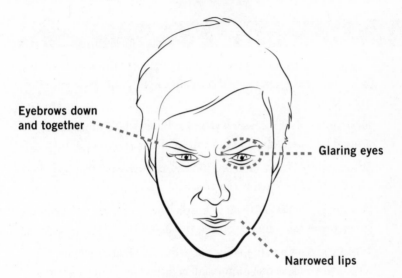

Eyebrows down and together

Glaring eyes

Narrowed lips

CONTEMPT

Exhibits a feeling of moral superiority or looking down on you, indicating that they have no respect for you.

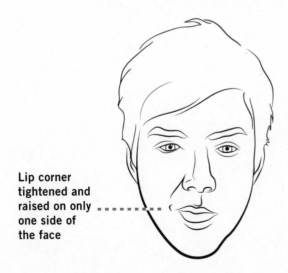

Lip corner tightened and raised on only one side of the face

Disgust, anger, and contempt or any combination of these three emotions is reason for concern.

TAKEAWAYS

- You always want to be scanning, or in a state of situational awareness, so that you can try to anticipate and respond to people or events.

- Head on a swivel and watch your six: know who and what is around you, including behind you, at all times.

- Scanning will alert you to pre-indicators, behaviors that help you know you are targeted for an attack.

- Scanning can also alert you to hostile and aggressive facial expressions so you can remove yourself to safety.

- When you have an adrenaline surge due to a flight-or-fight response, you lose fine motor skill abilities (such as using pepper spray or dialing a phone) but you gain gross motor skills, such as kicking, running, elbowing, and kneeing.

4
THE RED ZONE

. . . .

The Red Zone, as the period between September and Thanksgiving recess is sometimes called, is when freshman females are at the most vulnerable time in their lives for sexual assault. And for returning sophomores, it's the second-most vulnerable time in their lives.

A few years ago, as the number of high-profile sexual assaults on university campuses rose rapidly, *Inside Edition* approached me about doing a piece on a college campus to answer the question: Are college women too trusting? This social experiment had never been attempted on a college campus in the United States, according to *Inside Edition*. One of the reasons for the increase in assaults was believed to be that female college students were not careful enough and put themselves in unsafe situations by letting down their guard too quickly.

I carefully selected eight women leaving classroom buildings at a major university in New York State. I used a variety of ruses, and all of the women I picked allowed me into their cars and drove away with me. Had I actually been a predator, their safety would have been completely compromised. Although a small sample, this experiment supports statistics and word-of-mouth observations that college-age women, especially first- and second-year students, are easy targets for predators due to their unsuspicious and unsuspecting attitudes.

It was September and the fall term had just begun. Students carrying backpacks were hurrying across the quad to classes or to the library. I had placed myself on the side of one of the large parking lots that dotted campus. Selectively I scanned the women who were walking by. I identified the ones who were unaware of their surroundings, lost in thought, talking on cell phones, or even eating lunch on the go. I looked at posture and stride, getting into the predator mindset. Research shows that in sexual assault cases, looks and outfits are irrelevant. Whether she's tall or short or wearing a miniskirt or sweats, none of that matters. Predators are most often solely interested in a woman who presents as a soft target.

Many people did spot me as out of place and decades too old, even with my quick student disguise of a backpack, baseball hat, and knee-length shorts. But just as many didn't even bother giving me a second glance. Walking right past me, their gaze lowered, texting or emailing. Or with the ubiquitous buds in their ears—chatting on the phone, listening to music. Or some combination of the above.

Of the women who were distracted—and startled when I approached them—I managed to get eight out of eight to let me into their cars by simply saying, "Hey there, could you drop me off at the security gates so I could get some help here?" And motioning in a vague way, as if toward my stalled vehicle.

That was all it took to let a stranger into their car.

The Red Zone

Freshman year at college. You have spent the past four years of high school working toward this. All the late nights, studying for tests and writing papers while the rest of your family slept. The hours spent dutifully practicing an instrument, staying late for soccer, volunteering, working over the summer. Whenever it was that you began dreaming of going off to college, you have finally made it.

It is an exciting rite of passage, considered one of the first steps toward independence and adulthood. You will be creating lifelong friendships, socializing, going to parties, and following your dreams. The dorms are decorated with welcome banners and colorful balloons. Everyone is smiling and you are giddy with anticipation.

As welcome week and the activities continue, the importance of this new phase in your life is underscored by the warm and supportive reception given to incoming freshmen by the college administration. They tell you that few things are more worthy of celebration than the entry of a new class of students into the university. You will be praised as being part of the next generation of leaders. And you are given assurances that the professors, the staff, and the administration are there to advise, support, and guide you on your path to achieving your full potential.

Your parents, who have been at your side through thick and thin, who encouraged you to aim for the stars, are perhaps saddened to be leaving you alone, but also trusting that the college is a partner in helping you become successful. They believe, as most of us do, that the respected name and stellar reputation of a college mean that it is a safe place.

All of this is true. You are in an exciting period in life and you will have opportunities that you didn't know existed. What you will not see, however, on the websites and brochures, and what nobody will talk about during your first weeks there, is the fact that sexual violence on campuses is pervasive, especially during freshman and sophomore year.

An estimated 20 to 25 percent of undergraduate females experience rape or sexual assault through physical force, violence, or incapacitation during their four years at college. Think about it: that is one in four women.

The term *Red Zone* is taken from football, where it refers to the last twenty yards before the goal line, when the offense has a high probability of scoring a touchdown. It indicates that conditions exceed standard safety limits, warning defensive players to be on high alert.

The start of the academic year, usually early September through Thanksgiving, is also known as the Red Zone. In this case, it refers to the safety of female students at college. It is the time when a freshman female is most vulnerable to sexual assault. Yes, there is an officially recognized period when standard safety limits are breached and you are at an increased risk for sexual violence. The second-most dangerous time is during your sophomore year, during the same months.

This is not a hidden statistic, discussed in hushed tones behind closed doors, passed along by word of mouth among campus security, law enforcement, and the university administration. This is a publicly acknowledged, widespread, and important issue, so serious that in 2008, Congress voted unanimously to designate September as National Campus Safety Awareness Month. Colleges and universities even purchase sexual assault insurance, which is the second-most-common insurance claim, right after assault and battery.

The majority of these assaults occur between midnight and 6 a.m. on Saturday and during the early hours of Sunday morning. As an incoming freshman or even sophomore, you may not be used to being handed drink after drink, free of charge, with no one carding you. Off campus it would be the equivalent of some crazy dive bar. You'd expect the police to show up any minute and shut down a place with rampant underage drinking. But on campus is a different story.

Your fellow classmates have undergone a vetting process, of sorts, by the university. And it's logical to think that those around you are more like you than people you were with in high school. But that feeling can also cause you to trust someone who is still very much a stranger. It's also common to be homesick and stressed out. The sudden removal of the protective barrier of home, school, community, and friends is a drastic change. Combined with an array of back-to-back parties and social events, where consuming alcohol in massive quantities is considered a rite of passage and can help ease social anxiety, you are vulnerable to predators, especially upperclassmen. For the first time in your life, you are in a situation where you are the only one responsible for your safety.

Friend or Foe?

You know enough to be aware that sexual assault happens on campus. You might have heard about a friend of a friend who had a bad experience. At night, you never walk alone and always walk in well-lit areas. Maybe you are not the partying kind. Going to a big party with a punch bowl and keg doesn't appeal to you. You prefer hanging around in your dorm with a small group. You have even discussed looking out for each other at parties. You are prepared. You are aware. It could never happen to you.

Then you get a text from a male friend, the one who sits next to you in your history class, inviting you to a last-minute get-together. He's the guy who saves you a seat up front at each lecture. You don't know him very well but he seems nice enough, and your friends are coming, too. However, as discussed in Chapter 1, this person is basically a stranger to you. Yes, you know him, but only in a public context.

In college, it's not likely that you will be attacked by a random stranger who jumps out of the bushes or who hides behind cars in the parking lot.

Statistically, you need to be worried about the people you know. The person who is most likely to sexually assault or rape you will be someone familiar. You may go to classes with him, you may see him at parties, you may be connected through social media. It may even be someone you consider a friend. The Department of Justice reports that 90 percent of college women who have been sexually assaulted or raped knew their attackers.

As awareness of sexual assault on college campuses grows, research has focused on the types of men involved in these crimes. It is worth noting that sexual assault at schools is not primarily carried out by repeat offenders. Hundreds of conversations with college-age men and women over the last ten years and a recent study* have shown that these men can be roughly divided into three categories.

THE GOOD GUYS: This makes up most men and they are the ones who do the right thing, whether by intervening or exercising good judgment.

THE BAD GUYS: A limited selection of men who will offend and reoffend—includes serial rapists.

THE ON-THE-FENCE GUYS: These are the opportunists. They will take advantage of a woman if she is in a compromised state, such as drunk,

* Kevin M. Swartout, PhD, et al., "Trajectory Analysis of the Campus Serial Rapist Assumption," *JAMA Pediatrics*, published online July 13, 2015.

drugged, or passed out. This is supported by research indicating that one-third of college men admitted that they would rape a woman if they knew that nobody would ever find out and that there would be no consequences. A man in this group might also be acting under the influence of alcohol or drugs and will feel guilty afterward.

Only Green Means Go

Green = Healthy	Yes means yes.
	Each wants the other to be happy, applies to nonsexual issues as well. Partners are equally interested.
Yellow = Pressure	Lack of mutual respect, trying to change someone's mind. Saying things like "Try it once, for me" or "Try it, you'll like it."
	Not taking no for an answer.
Orange = Coercion	Using pressure (as in yellow) combined with threats to persuade their partner. For example, "If you don't do this, then I will tell everyone that you have an STD."

Red = Force

The definition of consent, meaning agreement at each stage of intimacy, has been evolving as schools grapple with ways to help and protect students. College campuses across the country have been adopting the notion of affirmative consent, meaning that only a freely given "yes" counts. Silence and indifference are not consent. If you are incapacitated due to drugs or alcohol, then you are not giving consent. Lack of protest or resistance does not mean consent. You should always remember that anyone who does not listen to and respect the two-letter word *no* has no respect for you and means to control you.

The notion of what constitutes agreement was first implemented at Antioch College in Ohio in 1993 when they introduced the slogan "Yes Means Yes."

Highlighting the difference in attitudes back then, *Saturday Night Live* initially mocked the rule in a skit featuring Phil Hartman as the host of a game show called *Is It Date Rape?* Actors mimed encounters that students (played by Shannen Doherty and Chris Farley) would judge as "date rape" or "not date rape."

As recently as 2011, "No Means No" has been used as fodder for offensive jokes. A Yale University fraternity was suspended for five years after its members marched around campus chanting, "No means yes, yes means anal!" during a pledge initiation event. A fraternity at Texas Tech was stripped of its charter after painting the same phrase on signs during a party.

Always remember that in any physical, sexual activity, all participants must give "affirmative and enthusiastic" consent at every step. If you cannot or do not, then you have not given your consent.

Get Your Act(s) Together

Get together with four of your closest female friends for lunch. Statistically, at least one of you will be sexually assaulted in college. Now look at eight women riding on a bus with you. Chances are that two of you will be assaulted. Your life changes forever after an assault. You don't just get up, brush yourself off, and hurry to class. The physical and emotional toll can take years to overcome. It can result in depression, anxiety, and self-harm. You may avoid men and sexual intimacy.

If one out of every four cars were stolen during the months of early September through Thanksgiving, it would warrant attention and outrage. There would be national awareness campaigns, public service messages, and full media coverage. The thieves would be hunted down and locked up. Private and government groups would work together to stop the car-stealing epidemic. While we don't yet have that type of response for sexual assault at schools, there are laws and acts in place to help and protect you. The two most important ones are the Clery Act and Title IX.

You may be wondering why colleges are even involved in sexual assault at all, since it is a criminal act that has nothing to do with education. Why not just report it to the police? Colleges and universities get involved in the process because access to education is considered a civil right and schools are required to make sure that all students have equal access to education, without violence or discrimination, which includes sexual conduct that could impede a student's ability to pursue her education. Reporting sexual assault to the school is not considered a replacement for reporting to the police; it is simply another option based on civil rights, rather than on criminal law.

The Clery Act

In 1986, Jeanne Clery, a sophomore at Lehigh University in Pennsylvania, awoke to find a fellow student robbing her dorm room. During the struggle that ensued, he beat, cut, raped, sodomized, and strangled her. The attack on her was one of thirty-eight attacks at the university over a three-year period, none of which had been publicly reported. The Clery family sued the university, arguing that, had they known about the university's crime record, they would not have sent their daughter there. As a result, the Jeanne Clery Disclosure of Campus Security Policy and Campus Crime Statistics Act was signed in 1990, stating that all colleges and universities, both public and private, that take part in federal financial aid programs are required to disclose information about crime on and near the campus. The information must be made publicly accessible through a school's Annual Security Report (ASR).

The incidents that must be reported include:

Criminal Offenses

- Criminal homicide (murder/nonnegligent manslaughter and manslaughter by negligence)
- Sexual assault (rape, fondling, incest, and statutory rape)
- Aggravated assault
- Burglary
- Motor vehicle theft
- Arson

Hate Crimes

Any of the above-mentioned crimes and any incidents of larceny—theft, simple assault, intimidation, or destruction/damage/vandalism of property that were motivated by bias.

Violence Against Women Act (VAWA) Offenses

- Domestic violence
- Dating violence
- Stalking

Arrests and Referrals for Disciplinary Action

- Weapons law violations (carrying, possessing, etc.)
- Drug abuse violations
- Liquor law violations

In addition, certain basic requirements for handling incidents of sexual assault, stalking, domestic violence, and dating violence are imposed. Compliance is monitored by the U.S. Department of Education and students can file complaints with them asking for their schools to be investigated for violations. Institutions that don't comply can be fined $27,500 per violation and fines can be levied for multiple violations per school. As of this writing, the largest penalty ever assessed against a single institution was nearly $2.4 million (Penn State, 2016).

Title IX

Title IX is considered a landmark amendment to the Civil Rights Act of 1964 and prohibits sex discrimination in education. You may be familiar with its importance in requiring gender equality in athletics, but it is much more than that. Regardless of gender or sexual orientation, it addresses sex-based discrimination at college. The purpose is to ensure that everyone has the opportunity to pursue education in a harassment-free environment. This includes any unwanted or unwelcome sexual behavior that significantly interferes with a student's access to educational opportunities. A student attending college where she has been assaulted can be considered to be in a hostile environment. Title IX is there to create a neutral environment. Title IX is very complex and institutions of higher education usually appoint a Title IX coordinator, frequently a lawyer, to ensure compliance.

Baylor University Scandal

Baylor University, in Texas, is one of the largest Baptist universities in the world and many of the families who send their sons and daughters there are seeking a sheltered collegiate environment for their kids. Drinking alcohol and premarital sex are banned by the Baylor student code of conduct.

Between 2012 and 2016, Baylor's football team came under fire when it was revealed that university officials failed to take action regarding alleged rapes and other assaults. Seventeen women reported sexual or domestic assaults involving nineteen players, including four alleged gang rapes.

The scandal led to the ouster of head football coach Art Briles, the demotion and eventual resignation of Baylor University president Ken Starr, the resignation of the athletic director, and the firing of two others connected with the football program. It also led to the resignation of the Title IX coordinator, Patty Crawford.

Crawford resigned after alleging that Baylor University did not allow her to do her job as Title IX coordinator properly. She claimed that the more she pushed to help the victims, the more resistance she felt from the board of advisors. She insisted that the board was full of "a group of seniors that made sure that they were protecting the brand instead of our students."

Baylor is also facing lawsuits from more than a dozen former students alleging the school turned a blind eye to reports of sexual assault over many years. The full impact of the damage caused by the broken campus model will not be completely known for years.

She Just Wants Justice

When there is sexual violence against a student on a university campus, the interests of the student and those of the university will usually diverge. While both the university and the student want a structure in place that provides emotional support and counseling and a path to healing, their long-term goals will frequently be different.

Although a student may not want to have the attention and notoriety associated with reporting a sexual assault, she will want the predator to be punished, whether he is suspended or expelled. Justice and responsibility and public acknowledgment are an important part of the healing process.

If a woman is directed or chooses to go to the women's center on campus, she will be provided with emotional support and counseling and given help to begin the healing process.

For the educational institution, its primary mission is to protect and preserve its brand. The university wants to continue to attract new students; it wants to maintain a strong alumni network, for both donations and to help recent graduates enter the workforce; and it wants all the hard-won accolades and honors it has received over the years to have meaning and value. The university will try to keep crime statistics as low as possible.

In order to maintain its reputation, a school can make it difficult for women to report sexual violence. A woman can be made to feel that she is the one who did something wrong and it is not uncommon for the administration to actively discourage women from going to the police so that there is no public record. It is estimated that fewer than 5 percent of females assaulted in college file a formal report or go to the police, though they may eventually tell a trusted friend.

This is also when the administrative process on a college campus could begin for the punishment of the offender. The criminal burden in a criminal prosecution is proof beyond a reasonable doubt. In a civil trial, the proof has to be the preponderance of evidence (tipping the scale, 51 percent to 49 percent).

Reporting a sexual assault to law enforcement is a personal decision. Sexual assault is not a crime subject to mandatory reporting, such as child abuse or neglect. It's a woman's choice whether or not to report it. The many complaints that I have heard about the bad models of dealing with sexual assault on university campuses is that often the administrative process is delayed, the accused party is left on campus and sometimes in the same classroom, the woman is blamed for the assault, or administrators drag their feet for so long that the accused is allowed to graduate. Some extreme examples of this are the incidents at Baylor University. That said, there are many good models that do their best to follow Title IX to the letter and to ensure justice is administered.

Involving law enforcement, the prosecutor's office, or the special victim unit of a branch of law enforcement will better ensure that the accused party is prosecuted and punished. Sexual assault cases are difficult to prosecute without proper evidence, however. If you do choose to report the crime to law enforcement, it is important to do so quickly so as not to lose physical proof. It is worth noting that if you are assaulted, in order to preserve valuable DNA evidence:

- You should not take a shower or wash up.
- You should not brush your teeth.
- You should not change your clothes.

Hair, fiber, and bodily fluids can confirm that a particular person was at a particular place. A forensic scientist can obtain a DNA profile through cells transferred to your body or ones present on a glass, clothing, or even a cigarette.

How Safe Is Your U?

The process of selecting a college should include considerations of safety and quality of life. Parents and prospective students will have a lot of questions for the college staff. The administrators, security, RAs, and the campus police should not only be prepared and have answers to your questions, but they should be willing to assist you in tracking down information they can't provide on the spot.

Six Tips for Selecting a Safe College

1. Visit the campus. You will experience it firsthand, see the layout, and get a gut feeling about it. Visit the student housing. Take a ride around the area surrounding the school. Some well-known campuses are located in the middle or on the outskirts of challenging settings. Parents and students should be familiar with the police departments, both on and off campus; the fire department; and hospitals and clinics, on and off campus.

2. Google news articles about the school and search for "[college or university name] sexual assault." See what comes up.

3. Read the school's Annual Security Report. Colleges and universities must publish this annual report every year by October 1. It contains three years' worth of Clery crime statistics (see pages 70–71) for the

campus, unobstructed public areas immediately adjacent to or running through the campus, and certain noncampus facilities including Greek housing and remote classrooms. You can visit this website to learn more about the topic: http://ope.ed.gov/security/. The ASR can be used to compare institutions and to review any trends at specific locations year over year.

4. Review the college website. Parents and prospective students should visit the school's website and review the available student resources, which should include counseling services, housing safety, Title IX information, emergency procedures, and more.

5. Enroll in mass notifications. Parents should urge students to opt in to the institution's mass notification system and to routinely provide current contact information.

6. Check local and national sex offender registries. Sex offender searches can be reviewed at the following site: https://www.fbi.gov/scams-and-safety/sex-offender-registry. This site and the local site can provide information on where they live and what level of sex offender they are.

Don't Be Too Trusting (Yes, That Means You)

When you read the title of this section, you might be tempted to blow it off as advice meant for someone else. Too trusting? You know how to take care of yourself. You would never get into a stranger's car, you would never let a stranger into your dorm, you won't walk home alone from the library late at night. You are not that naïve girl who gets so drunk at a party that she spends most of the night throwing up in the bathroom. Not your scene.

Before you decide to skip to the next section, take a moment to read the quiz below and note how many statements ring true.

Self-Assessment: How Trusting Am I?

1. If I disagree with someone, I'd rather agree to disagree or compromise.

2. I'm in an exciting period in my life and don't mind taking a few extra risks.

3. People behave pretty much as I expect them to.

4. I consider myself free-spirited and spontaneous, able to respond quickly to situations when they arise.

5. I pride myself on being kind and helpful, giving people the benefit of the doubt.

6. I would be uncomfortable being rude and yelling: "No" or "Stay back" or "Stay away."

If you agreed with one or more of these, then you may be too trusting.

As a frequent guest speaker at colleges and universities around the country, I cover many topics that affect students, such as sexual harassment, sexual abuse, sexual assault, alcohol, and date rape, yet few subjects cause as much reaction among the audience as the way upperclassmen shamelessly talk about targeting first- and second-year students. It is an open secret. Incoming females are considered "fresh meat."

Some upperclassmen have no qualms about getting them drunk, drugged, whatever it takes, with the goal of sexual conquest. Research* and interviews have made it clear that male students who are two or three years older than the freshmen consciously choose women who they know will be easy to take advantage of. These women are excited to be at college, may be away from home for the first time, they don't know much about how alcohol will affect them, they want to be invited to parties, and, if they are involved in the Greek system, they like the idea of having a group of older brothers.

When you get to college, you will interact with fellow students who are two or three years older than you. There will be no easy way to tell if any of them are sexual predators, but they will all be strangers. No matter how many classes you take together, in a dating or partying scenario, they should be treated as strangers. Your experience with them and your expectations of how they act and behave have been confined to the classroom or parties with other friends.

* David Lisak, associate professor of psychology at the University of Massachusetts Boston and director of the Men's Sexual Trauma Research Center, has done extensive research in this field and has released an enlightening video called *The Undetected Rapist*.

In psychology, the façade that people put up when you first get to know them is referred to as the front stage. When you are meeting new people, especially when alcohol is involved, you are seeing their front stage. Maybe they are charming and attentive and funny. Once you really get to know them, then you are seeing their back stage. Everyone has a front stage and back stage. Men know that mentioning things that you have in common, such as a favorite show or music or gaming, or trying to sell you on the fact that they have great relationships with their mother or sisters, or talking about mutual friends will get you to relax. But this does not actually reveal what type of person they are.

Be kind, be friendly, but be cautious with new friendships and relationships.

Think Before You Drink

Margaret loved freshman year at college. She liked her roommates and met lots of people. The football team had just won a game and Margaret and her friends went to an off campus party to celebrate. At about 10 p.m., a frantic 911 call was made about an unconscious girl. I was the first officer to arrive and found a big, burly football player with a frightened look on his face. He was holding a limp, unconscious girl around her waist as she purged vomit into a fifty-five-gallon garbage can. I suspected he'd never seen this before, but I knew that her condition was very serious. An ambulance rushed her to the hospital. Her blood alcohol level, meaning the amount of alcohol circulating in her body, was so high that she was admitted to the ICU and was in the hospital for two days.

How much do you have to drink to get yourself hospitalized for forty-eight hours, in the ICU no less?

Margaret's blood alcohol level was about .22 percent, half of what would kill a mature adult. Her drink of choice was a mixture that was equal parts Gatorade and 80-proof whiskey. She became highly intoxicated and passed out. Her friends were going to drive her back to the dorm, but they noticed that she just didn't look right and was having trouble breathing. Luckily for her, that's when the police were called. Due to her low tolerance and lack of experience with drinking, the amount of alcohol she had in her system very nearly killed her. Had her friends taken her back to her dorm and left her to sleep it off, she would not have made it. Elevated levels of blood alcohol cause the medulla, the part of the brain that controls your body temperature, your heart, and your breathing, to stop working.

While drinking may ease social anxiety and help you relax after studying hard, women may end up paying a high price by choosing alcohol. It affects women differently than men due to the naturally varying levels of muscle and fat tissue, all of which metabolize alcohol at different rates. The following chart illustrates how just one drink can rapidly alter a woman's behavior while a man's body can tolerate higher amounts before being affected.

Drinking at colleges has become a ritual that is seen as an integral part of higher education. Many students arrive at school with established drinking habits, and the easy access to beer and mixed drinks can exacerbate the problem. According to a national survey, almost 60 percent of college students ages eighteen to twenty-two drank alcohol in the past month. Close to two out of three engaged in binge drinking during that same time.

Mentally, alcohol makes you less inhibited and clouds your judgment. Men who are looking for a night of sexual conquest may overlook you for a softer target if you are sober and alert. Once you take a drink, you are an easy target for a sexual predator. When you are buzzed or drunk, you are automatically a target. The most harmful consequences as a result of excessive alcohol consumption are death, assault, and sexual assault.

Alcohol Makes You a Target

As a former police officer, I'd love to tell you not to drink or take drugs, especially during the Red Zone, to avoid being selected by a predator. But I know that's not realistic. However, you should keep in mind that the consumption of alcohol, even small amounts, will cause decreased inhibition, making you likely to do something or engage in an activity that you may not have otherwise done. Loss of inhibitions can also lead to a false sense of confidence or engaging in risky behavior.

As a central nervous system depressant, alcohol slows down your reaction time. The more you drink, the less you are going to be able to deal with a compromising situation, such as reacting to someone who doesn't take no for an answer. Your ability to resist and physically fight back will diminish with each sip. Ingesting high amounts will cause emotional instability, loss of critical judgment, impairment of perception, and decreased sensory response.

I hope that the knowledge that during the first two years of college you are at a high risk for sexual assault by a fellow classmate will lead you to minimize your alcohol consumption.

Consider the stats:

DEATHS: Approximately 1,800 college students between the ages of eighteen and twenty-four die each year from alcohol-related accidental injuries, including falls and car crashes.

ASSAULTS: More than 600,000 students between the ages of eighteen and twenty-four are assaulted each year by another student who has been drinking.

SEXUAL ASSAULTS: Nearly 100,000 students between the ages of eighteen and twenty-four experience alcohol- and/or drug-facilitated sexual assaults and/or date rapes.

ALCOHOL IMPAIRMENT CHART

MALE

DRINKS*	BODY WEIGHT IN POUNDS								EFFECTS ON PERSON
	100	120	140	160	180	200	220	240	
0	0.00	0.00	0.00	0.00	0.00	0.00	0.00	0.00	ONLY SAFE DRIVING LIMIT
1	0.04	0.03	0.03	0.02	0.02	0.02	0.02	0.02	IMPAIRMENT BEGINS
2	0.08	0.06	0.05	0.05	0.04	0.04	0.03	0.03	
3	0.11	0.09	0.08	0.07	0.06	0.06	0.05	0.05	DRIVING SKILLS SIGNIFICANTLY AFFECTED
4	0.15	0.12	0.11	0.09	0.08	0.08	0.07	0.06	
5	0.19	0.16	0.13	0.12	0.11	0.09	0.09	0.08	
6	0.23	0.19	0.16	0.14	0.13	0.11	0.10	0.09	LEGALLY INTOXICATED
7	0.26	0.22	0.19	0.16	0.15	0.13	0.12	0.11	
8	0.30	0.25	0.21	0.19	0.17	0.15	0.14	0.13	CRIMINAL PENALTIES IN ALL STATES**
9	0.34	0.28	0.24	0.21	0.19	0.17	0.15	0.14	
10	0.38	0.31	0.27	0.23	0.21	0.19	0.17	0.16	

FEMALE

DRINKS*	BODY WEIGHT IN POUNDS									EFFECTS ON PERSON
	90	100	120	140	160	180	200	220	240	
0	0.00	0.00	0.00	0.00	0.00	0.00	0.00	0.00	0.00	ONLY SAFE DRIVING LIMIT
1	0.05	0.05	0.04	0.03	0.03	0.03	0.02	0.02	0.02	IMPAIRMENT BEGINS
2	0.10	0.09	0.08	0.07	0.06	0.05	0.05	0.04	0.04	DRIVING SKILLS SIGNIFICANTLY AFFECTED
3	0.15	0.14	0.11	0.11	0.09	0.08	0.07	0.06	0.06	
4	0.20	0.18	0.15	0.13	0.11	0.10	0.09	0.08	0.08	
5	0.25	0.23	0.19	0.16	0.14	0.13	0.11	0.10	0.09	
6	0.30	0.27	0.23	0.19	0.17	0.15	0.14	0.12	0.11	LEGALLY INTOXICATED
7	0.35	0.32	0.27	0.23	0.20	0.18	0.16	0.14	0.13	
8	0.40	0.36	0.30	0.26	0.23	0.20	0.18	0.17	0.15	CRIMINAL PENALTIES IN ALL STATES**
9	0.45	0.41	0.34	0.29	0.26	0.23	0.2	0.19	0.17	
10	0.50	0.45	0.38	0.32	0.28	0.25	0.23	0.21	0.19	

Subtract .01% for each 40 minutes of drinking.

* One drink is equal to 1¼ ounces of 80-proof liquor, 12 ounces of beer, or 4 ounces of table wine.
** As of October 2004, all states were mandated by federal law to institute a .08 blood alcohol content (BAC) law or face losing federal highway construction funds.

WHAT YOU DON'T LEARN IN HEALTH ED: The chart opposite is for an adult. The amount needed to cause intoxication in a young adult or teenager may be only half of that needed for a mature adult. Similarly, as was the case with Margaret, acute alcohol poisoning can occur in a young adult or teenager at rates half of those of an adult.

ABSORPTION: Alcohol makes it into your bloodstream quickly. Trace amounts are absorbed in the mouth, approximately 10 to 20 percent is absorbed in the stomach, and 75 to 80 percent is absorbed in the small intestine.

BODY WEIGHT AND BODY TYPE: In general, the less you weigh, the more you will be affected by alcohol (see chart opposite). Moreover, alcohol has a high affinity for water. In the case of two individuals with similar body compositions and different weights, the larger individual will achieve lower alcohol concentrations than the smaller one when they ingest the same amount of alcohol. However, for people of the same weight, a well-muscled individual will be less affected than someone with a higher percentage of fat, since fatty tissue does not contain very much water and will not absorb very much alcohol.

GENDER DIFFERENCES: In general, but not in all cases, women tend to have a higher percentage of body fat and thus a lower percentage of body water. Therefore, if a man and a woman of the same weight ingest the same amount of alcohol, generally the woman will tend to achieve a higher alcohol concentration. This, of course, would change if the woman were very fit and the man were somewhat obese, but on average, this is the case. Furthermore, total body water tends to decrease with age, so an older person will also be more affected by the same amount of alcohol.

FOOD: To prevent the most harmful consequences, it's best to eat right before drinking. Alcohol in the stomach is absorbed more slowly and less efficiently than in the small intestine. When you eat, the small intestine will first digest the food, holding the alcohol in your stomach longer, slowing down its absorption by the body.

The pyloric valve at the bottom of the stomach will close in order to hold food in the stomach for digestion and thus keep the alcohol from reaching the small intestine. While alcohol will be absorbed from the stomach, it is a slower and less efficient transition.

FATIGUE: Fatigue will amplify the effects of alcohol. If you have pulled an all-night cramming session and go to a party after the test to celebrate, the effects of the alcohol may be increased.

MEDICATION: Many medications, including over-the-counter drugs for cold and flu, can enhance the effects of alcohol. Drugs used to treat ADHD, such as Ritalin, may mask the depressant effects of alcohol and make you less aware that your judgment and physical reactions are impaired, because they are stimulants.

DEHYDRATION: Excess alcohol consumption can cause dehydration in a variety of ways, but if you drink after a big workout, the effects will be enhanced if you have not replenished your fluids. The less water in the body, the more concentrated the alcohol will be.

Never Leave a Friend Behind

Go out as a group, go home as a group: a simple concept and one of the fundamental rules to staying safe. Ideally, you will have one person watching over your group of three to five friends (anything more becomes difficult to manage), and you will all agree in advance on the time when you will go home together. This is especially important at a large party with people you don't know and where there will probably be drugs and alcohol.

In the perfect world, the people you meet during freshman year will be your close friends until the end of college. They will be your support system and look out for you at parties. In the real world, the people you meet during freshman or sophomore year at college will probably not end up being long-term friends. You are more vulnerable during these two years partially due to the lack of a trusted support system and social network.

The next chapter will give you detailed tips and strategies you can use when going out.

Date Rape Drugs

Date rape drugs are colorless, odorless, and tasteless drugs that can be secretly added to your drink. You will not know that you have been drugged and it will be easy for a sexual predator to take advantage of you. The best defense is to always watch your drink and keep an eye on your friends. The next chapter will go into detail on how to protect yourself in social situations from date rape drugs and predators.

SELF-AWARENESS QUIZ

How Do You View the Guys at School?

#1. All of them are cool.

#2. Most of them are nice, a few are creepy.

If you think they are all cool, then you need to practice being on guard and using your intuition.

If you think most are nice and a few are creepy, you are ahead of the game.

Always Fight Back

No matter what the circumstances, if you find yourself being pressured or physically coerced into any type of sexual activity at all, always fight back. Chapter 7 details how to fight back effectively. A high percentage of the cases I have investigated and studied indicate that if a woman fights back, and fights back effectively, she can prevail with little or no injury. Even though you may imagine that by giving in, it will be over faster, that is not necessarily the case. By fighting back, you make yourself less desirable and more challenging to manage. You may also believe that by fighting back you will provoke and anger your attacker. But just by taking a stand you will often demotivate a would-be assailant.

Statistics show that in sexual assault cases you will know your attacker 70 to 75 percent of the time (friend, acquaintance, relative). If you're attending college, 90 percent of the time you will know your attacker, according to a study conducted by the U.S. Department of Justice. It will not be the masked man jumping out of the bushes. It will likely be someone you see on a regular basis.

In cases like these, known as acquaintance assault, de-escalation techniques and fighting back can be very effective. Frequently your attacker is an opportunist, one of the on-the-fence guys, taking advantage of a situation where he thinks he can get away with it. You will have things in common, such as friends or classes, and he knows he will see you around. He may also be drunk or high and will regret his actions the next day. When you try to talk him out of it or put up a fight, all of these factors come into play and can work in your favor.

You may find yourself alone with someone who is sexually aggressive. Or you may be in a dorm room, isolated, and your intuition tells you something is wrong. As soon as you can, try to make your exit. The following statements can create a break in your interactions. He may think it is only temporary, but you should be prepared to run or use your phone to call for help. If one of these doesn't work, keep on trying. Never give up.

1. Hold on a second, my mom had surgery this afternoon and I promised I would call. Just give me a minute. (Utilize the time to make a call for help or make your escape.)

2. You have beer breath. Would you mind brushing your teeth?

3. I'm allergic to your cologne.

4. My roommate will be walking in any minute now.

5. My stomach hurts, I think I'm going to be sick. (Run to the bathroom or out of the dorm room.)

6. Hey, my friends (or family) know that we're hanging out together.

If you have tried to talk him out of it and he is still persistent, use all your energy to physically fight back. Make it hard for him.

Get Involved

A few years ago, a YouTube video called "Snack Man," filmed on the subway in Manhattan, went viral. A female rider got into a physical altercation with a guy she accused of following her. Punches and kicks were thrown. A young man heading uptown to meet friends felt compelled to do something. While munching on Pringles and gummy bears, he walked between the man and woman and started chewing. Immediately the fighting ceased. This is a perfect example of how getting involved can change the dynamics of a tense situation. Regardless of what is going on, the insertion of a few words such as "Is everything okay here?" or "Is there anything I can do to help?" can prevent or defuse trouble. Normally people don't want to fight and will look for any excuse to avoid or stop one.

By being an active bystander, you can thwart conflict and sexual assault. For example, at a party you may see a friend being led away into a bedroom or you may see a man accompanying a woman to the bathroom. If she seems incapacitated, then she is unable to consent to being isolated with a man. You can intervene by saying, "Hey, I need to talk to her for a minute," or "Can I talk to you for a second?" or even "Hey, do you realize how drunk she is?"

If the situation is overwhelming, solicit the help of others or call an RA or the police. Do not feel scared or awkward about reaching out for help. But most important, do something.

Spring Break Safety Tips

Looking forward to your break of nonstop fun, socializing, clubbing, beaching it, drinking, and letting loose? Heading to one of the hotspots like Las Vegas, Miami, or Cancún?

While spring break is a fun rite of passage for thousands of students, things can quickly turn dangerous or deadly if you don't take steps to protect yourself.

The greatest dangers during spring break are associated with binge drinking. Binge drinking occurs when a male consumes five or more drinks in two hours or a woman consumes four or more drinks in a two-hour period. The end result is an increase in unintentional injuries (car crashes, falls, drownings) and intentional injuries (through the use of firearms, assault, sexual assault, domestic violence), alcohol poisoning, sexually transmitted diseases, and unintended pregnancies.

To be safe, be sure to do your homework and research your destination. Anticipating problems before they happen and having a plan or solution in place can and will save you grief later on. While traveling, and once you get there, stay alert and be aware of who and what is around you.

It doesn't matter where you go. If you drop your guard, there will be someone willing to take advantage. And as much as spring break is known around college campuses, it is also known by predators as a good place to find soft targets.

Here are your spring break checklists to stay safe.

Spring Break Checklist

Travel

☐ Make a list of the essentials you will need on your trip. Travel as light as you possibly can; lots of luggage can be distracting and make you a target for theft.

☐ Keep your valuables out of sight and in your carry-on or backpack or on your person.

☐ Don't keep all of your credit cards and cash in one place.

☐ Know how you will get to your hotel from the airport. Arrange for your transportation before you arrive. You will be overwhelmed by legitimate and illegitimate drivers; they know you are coming.

☐ When using Uber or Lyft, you will see the driver's name, license plate number, car description, and photo on your phone when you request the ride. Verify this information when your car arrives.

☐ If you are using a shuttle service, watch your luggage get loaded onto the shuttle.

- [ ] All genuine taxis will have some sort of ID or badge. You can check for this before accepting a ride.

- [ ] If you are carrying a backpack, arrange your zippers to one side and not in the center so that the zipper has to be fully opened. You can use a small lock, but that's a giveaway that you are carrying something of value. I prefer a small zip tie with the end cut off.

- [ ] When walking through heavily traveled transportation hubs, have your head on a swivel and scan while on the go.

- [ ] Thieves love the chaos of an airport, subway, bus terminal, or busy resort.

Once You Arrive at the Hotel

- [ ] Don't give your personal information to the clerk. Hand over your license and credit card. The less anyone knows about you the better.

- [ ] Ask the clerk to write down your room number so that other people at check-in don't hear what room you are staying in.

- [ ] Grab a hotel business card and confirm the address. Take the card with you or take a snapshot with your cell phone.

- [ ] Become familiar with the layout of the hotel.

- [ ] Reserve a room between the second and seventh floors so it is within reach of a fire department ladder.

- [ ] Use the room safe for your extra cash and valuables.

- [ ] Make a copy of your passport, driver's license, travel documents, and credit cards. Keep the copies in the safe.

- [ ] Request a room away from the stairs, elevators, and vending machines.

- [ ] Don't assume that your room will have a dead bolt or secure lock. Pack an adjustable door security bar or a doorjamb/stop for while you are in your room. You can google these; they are made by all the major lock manufacturers.

- [ ] Check your room to ensure the windows and any adjoining room doors are secure.

☐ Post the DO NOT DISTURB sign when you go out and leave the TV on low volume, especially in the evening hours.

While at the ATM

☐ Always pay close attention to the ATM and your surroundings. Scan the area before you approach the ATM and maintain awareness of your surroundings throughout the transaction.

☐ Use your hand to cover the keyboard when entering your PIN.

☐ Never count cash at the machine or in public. Wait until you are in your car or in your hotel room.

☐ Closely monitor your bank statements, as well as your balances, and immediately report any problems to your bank.

While on the Beach

☐ No lifeguard, no lifeline. Don't go into the water without a lifeguard present.

☐ Know the flag system for water safety:

> *Red flag: Stay out of the water because of strong undertow and riptides.*

> *Yellow flag: Use caution in the water. There are some undertow and riptides possible. Also, ocean predators may be listed.*

> *Blue flag: Calm water. Swim safely.*

☐ Educate yourself about riptides and always swim parallel with the beach if you feel yourself being pulled out into the ocean.

☐ If you have been drinking and you encounter a problem in the water, you will be much slower to respond and try to solve it.

☐ Alcohol can dilate blood vessels and lower blood pressure to dangerous levels. The effects of alcohol are felt quicker and more intensely in a hot tub and can lead to unconsciousness and drowning.

Spring Break Abroad

☐ If you're leaving the country, you'll need a passport issued by the U.S. Department of State. You can find information at travel.state.gov.

☐ You can check the Travel Warnings section on the State Department website and you can also enroll in the Smart Traveler Enrollment Program (STEP) at step.state.gov and receive alerts and announcements.

☐ Make two photocopies of the front and back of all cards, travel documents, and passports and leave with family or a close friend and leave the second copy in the safe in your room. If your documents are stolen or lost, this will make canceling cards much easier.

☐ Be sure to have the contact information for the nearest U.S. embassy or consulate. They can provide assistance twenty-four hours a day, seven days a week.

☐ Be aware of local scam artists by doing an Internet search for your destination using keywords related to scams. There are a number of government and private sites that will be helpful.

☐ If you are robbed, your belongings can be replaced but you cannot.

☐ Does your health insurance cover you outside the United States? If not, consider purchasing a short-term policy that does.

☐ Carry more medications than you will need, keep them in the original containers, and obtain a letter from your doctor explaining your medical condition and the generic names of the medications you are taking.

☐ Check and understand the exchange rate before you leave for your destination.

☐ Do not take shortcuts. Stay on well-traveled streets.

☐ Check your phone before you leave the United States to be sure that you are enabled to use it overseas in case of an emergency.

☐ Many common overseas spring break destinations do not use 911 in case of emergencies. Be sure to obtain the correct information and store it in your phone.

TAKEAWAYS

- One in four women experience rape or sexual assault in college.
- You are most at risk for sexual assault during the fall of your freshman year and the fall of your sophomore year, a season known as the Red Zone.
- 90 percent of college women who have been raped or sexually assaulted know their attacker.
- Drinking alcohol makes you a target for rape or sexual assault.
- Never leave a friend behind.
- Get involved; use de-escalation techniques.
- Always fight back.

5
SOCIAL SITUATIONS

██████████

It was Saturday night and Laurie, a twenty-year-old college sophomore, was out with a bunch of dorm mates at a big party. Across the room she spied Ted, a junior she'd met through mutual friends, walking toward her with a glass of punch. They'd had a couple of dates before and she liked him, but the relationship had not been intimate. She was happy to see someone she knew and took the drink with a smile. After that, her mind went blank. She had no recollection of what happened next or how the night ended.

The next morning, she was all banged up and had bruises on her body that she couldn't explain. Ted's response to her text about the evening made her feel even worse: "We had a great time. You got pretty drunk and were so funny. I can't believe you don't remember." She was left with a bad feeling but couldn't figure out what had happened. She had never blacked out before, yet that was the only plausible explanation she could come up with. She went to classes on Monday and fell back into her routine, though her gut feeling that something was wrong persisted. She saw Ted on campus and he'd always smile and say hello but they never exchanged any words.

Six weeks later she tested positive in a pregnancy test, even though to her knowledge she hadn't been sexually active for months. With one of her best friends, she put together a timeline and puzzled the pieces together. A man she had trusted, a person who knew her friends, had given her a date rape drug and sexually assaulted her. She never reported the incident to the college administration or to the police.

The Golden Rules of Going Out

Going out to a bar or a club, whether with one friend or with a group, can seem like the perfect way to take a break and enjoy yourself. You get to dress up, hang out with people you like, listen to music, relax with a drink or two, dance (if that's your thing), and maybe in the process even meet someone new. While becoming uninhibited and letting your guard down can seem like part of the fun, a location with people you don't know and where alcohol and drugs are present is also the perfect environment for a predator to make a move. These Golden Rules will add a layer of protection, making you a hard target.

SAFETY IN NUMBERS. Always go out as a group and come home as a group. The best size is one made up of three to five people; anything bigger than that is hard to handle. Keep track of your friends and try to stick together, or at least in pairs. You should agree in advance on what to look for and what to do if it seems that one of you has been drugged.

Ideally, you will have a designated "mom" for the night. This will be the friend who has the group's updated contact info, who turns up her cell phone volume really loud, especially if you separate, who tries to keep an eye on how much people are drinking, and who corrals everyone together at the end of the night. She will also watch for any stranger or acquaintance who is trying to lure away members of your group.

WATCH YOUR DRINK AT ALL TIMES. Date rape drugs, such as GHB, are colorless, odorless, and tasteless. They can be easily slipped into your glass, and without knowing it, you can become incapacitated and easy to take advantage of. Sip out of bottles if possible. If you are going to the ladies' room, your drink goes with you. If you are going to the dance floor, so does your drink. Always have your drink in view or cover it with your hand if you turn your head.

OUT FOR THE NIGHT? PACK LIGHT. Have a small purse or evening bag dedicated for when you go out at night. Large purses are hard to keep an eye on in a club or at a party, making them easier to steal. Be sure to bring your cell phone, a photo ID, cash, and a credit card. Leave extra money, change, additional cards, and keys at home.

KNOW HOW YOU'RE GETTING HOME. Don't go out with a plan to wing it to get home safely. Add the number of the local taxi service into your phone or use Uber or Lyft rather than hailing a cab on the street. Never accept a ride from a stranger, even if you have spent the whole evening talking to him. And never give a stranger a ride home.

LISTEN TO YOUR INTUITION. If a person or situation feels wrong and you don't feel comfortable, trust your gut and leave. Go to a different place or go home. There will always be another night to go out.

HOW WELL CAN YOU IDENTIFY A COULD-BE RAPIST IN A SOCIAL SETTING?

True or False:

Rapists tend to be good-looking and think they should get what they want.

Rapists tend to be men who are sexually frustrated.

Rapists seldom have sisters, since they'd be more sensitive to women if they did.

Guys involved in aggressive sports are more likely to be rapists.

Answers appear on page 110.

Sexual predators actively utilize several tactics to make you feel comfortable around them and to drop your guard. One of their goals will be to find something in common with you, giving you a false sense of security. Once you relax and are less careful, it will be easier for them to take advantage.

Alcohol + Alcohol = Dangerous Combination

Alcohol tops the list as the most frequently used drug in sexual assault. In the previous chapter, I covered the effects of alcohol on your system.

One of the oldest tricks in the book is to add a shot of vodka to a glass of beer. It can more than double your blood alcohol level and is very difficult to detect. You likely will not notice any difference in smell or taste, especially if you have consumed one beer already. You may think you have had two or three beers while it may be closer to four or six. This is a very dangerous mix.

Drug-Facilitated Sexual Assault

If you're out on a date or at a party or club and you hear names like Swirl, Special K, Liquid E, Scoop, Blue Nitro, Forget Pill, Roofies, or Fantasy, then date rape drugs may be around and in use. Even worse, they may be in your drink.

Some predators use these drugs to facilitate a sexual assault. They will be slipped into your drink without your knowledge or consent. You will not be able to tell that you are drugged and you will be incapacitated. You may feel drowsy, confused, or physically weak or go into a state of unconsciousness. There can be serious side effects, such as respiratory difficulty, low blood pressure, suppression of the gag reflex, coma, and even death. Your memory will be affected. When the drug wears off, you may not be able to recall whom you were with, what you did, or where you were.

If a date rape drug is secretly added to your glass, then you will be left defenseless and at the mercy of a predator. You will not be able to resist or even call for help. It will be easy for him to steer you to a secluded location where you will most likely be sexually assaulted. There is absolutely no reason why a stranger would introduce one of these drugs into your drink, without your permission, other than with bad intentions. Drugging another person without their knowledge or consent is a crime, as is having sex with someone who is incapacitated or unconscious to the point that they can't give their consent because they are drugged, drunk, passed out, or asleep.

Moreover, you will not be able to provide law enforcement with the information needed to investigate and prosecute such an assault because either you will not remember anything or your memory will be blurry.

Getting your drink spiked with a date rape drug can happen anywhere drinking occurs, with alcoholic and nonalcoholic beverages. The perfect environments are clubs, bars, pubs, raves, restaurants, and large parties— any location where there are large groups of people and where it can be difficult to watch your drink at all times.

Date Rape Drugs Are Not Just for Clubs

Jennifer, a twenty-eight-year-old professional, worked in the marketing division of a major corporation. She was attending the company Christmas party solo for the first time. As she was having her last glass of wine and thinking about going home, she ran into her boss of three years and they began to chat. She asked him to keep an eye on her drink as she visited the ladies' room. When she returned, a few coworkers had joined them and she stayed for some additional small talk. Getting ready to grab her coat, she began to feel dizzy and nauseous. Her boss guided her over to a chair and she sat for a few minutes but only felt worse. He suggested that they head up to his office, where it was quieter and she could have a glass of ice water. Walking toward his office was the last thing she remembered.

The next day she awoke in her bed wearing a night shirt and her underpants. Next to her was a note from one of her female friends and coworkers, Lauren, letting her know that she had been driven home by her and the boss. Another female coworker, Carol, had driven her car to her condo complex. Lauren and Carol helped her get undressed and into bed. Jennifer had no recollection of the night's events, but she did remember having a third glass of wine. As a regular wine drinker, she knew her limits and wasn't even close with three glasses.

As the days went on, she started having flashbacks. She would see her boss on top of her on his office couch and she remembered having trouble breathing. These flashbacks resulted in her having anxiety and panic attacks.

Generally, only a small amount of a date rape drug is needed to cause impairment. When combined with alcohol, either because the drug is surreptitiously slipped directly into your drink or because you've had one drink already and alcohol is in your system, its adverse efficacy is magnified. A variety of other factors influence how these drugs can affect you. They include the potency and dose amount, and whether it is mixed with other drugs.

Date rape drugs are commonly transported in liquid form in small containers such as the plastic bottles used for eye drops, contact lens solution, nasal spray, and mouthwash. Their diminutive size makes them easy to conceal in a jacket pocket and facilitates the unobtrusive squirting of a dose into an open container. Moreover, a man carrying around a bottle of Visine will not draw any interest or comment. Not as frequently, date rape drugs are available in powdered form.

If you hear people joking about spiking a drink or punch bowl, do something. Warn other people at the party and throw your drink away. If someone seems very drunk, gets sick or is having trouble breathing and can't be awakened, or is behaving in some other unusual way, get medical help.

The Predator's Drug of Choice: GHB

GHB (gamma hydroxybutyrate) has become the predator's current favorite date rape drug. It is usually available in liquid form, and only a very small amount, as little as a capful, is needed to create an intoxicating effect along with amnesia. It is easily made in home laboratories with recipes just a mouse click away. Although available in health food stores in the late 1980s to enhance muscle tone and build strength and assist in the muscle recovery process, it was banned by the FDA in 1990 due to instances of respiratory distress and death of some users.

It is also referred to as G Scoop, Jib, Liquid E, Liquid X, Grievous Body Harm, Easy Lay, Salty Water, Women's Viagra, Swirl, and the Date Rape Drug.

Symptoms vary widely depending on dose and concentration. It is a fast-acting central nervous system depressant and onset can begin in as little as five minutes and last between three and six hours. You may start feeling euphoric, have a burst of energy and a loss of inhibitions, and experience increased sexual excitement, and then you may start slurring your speech, lose muscle control, vomit, and pass out. You may be functional and possibly awake, but you may not remember what occurred.

GHB has a very low margin separating a tolerable amount of the drug and a potentially fatal dose. Anyone who exceeds what may be considered a safe dose is at a very high risk for more severe side effects and an accidental overdose. An overdose can cause diminished respiratory function, in turn leading to respiratory distress, possibly respiratory arrest, and ultimately death. The gag reflex can be severely affected and cause a person to choke on their vomit.

Common Signs of a GHB Overdose

- Vomiting
- Loss of the gag reflex
- Shaking and seizures
- Loss of consciousness
- Profuse sweating
- Lowered body temperature
- Respiratory distress

As with most date rape drugs, you will suffer from amnesia and may not be able to recall what happened to you while you were under the influence of this drug. Again, these symptoms are greatly enhanced when mixed with alcohol.

Most of the GHB on the market today is homemade. It is made by nonprofessionals in their own labs, kitchens, or bathtubs. The purity and potency of a dose are inconsistent due to the amateur manufacture of the drug. This makes it all the more dangerous because doses of a similar size can have very different effects, depending on who made them.

GHB may have a salty taste that people sometimes try to mask by mixing it with a sweet liqueur or fruit juice.

The body metabolizes GHB rapidly and four to twelve hours later it may not be detected in the bloodstream. The body also produces GHB, further complicating detection.

Ketamine

Synthesized in the 1960s as an anesthetic for both human and animal use, ketamine is a hallucinogenic drug similar to PCP (phencyclidine). In a medical setting, it is used to treat chronic pain and provides sedation in intensive care.

Common street names are Special K, K, or Vitamin K. Intentional users refer to the high caused by ketamine as the K-hole and describe a hallucination that includes visual distortion and lost sense of time and identity. A single dose is sometimes referred to as a "bump."

Users report a dreamy feeling and the sensation that they are floating outside their body. Numbness of the extremities is also common. As with GHB, the initial high gives way to amnesia and you will be unable to give details of a sexual assault. When introduced into a beverage, the effects begin in about fifteen to twenty minutes and the amnesia may last for one to two hours. One of the side effects is flashbacks, which can occur for up to two weeks. The drug may be detectable in the body for up to twenty-four hours.

Ketamine usually comes as a liquid in a small pharmaceutical bottle and is most often cooked into a white powder for snorting by intentional users. The drug can also be injected or placed into a beverage, usually alcohol.

Veterinary hospitals are a major source of ketamine through burglaries. Sometimes the only thing missing in a burglary will be injectable bottles of liquid ketamine.

The Original Date Rape Drug: Rohypnol

Rohypnol is the trade name for flunitrazepam, a drug in the same family of medications as Valium and Xanax. Up to ten times as powerful as Valium, it was first marketed to the public in 1974 to help with insomnia. It is also used as an anesthetic and can be administered in surgeries where the patient may have to respond or cooperate. However, it has never been approved for use in the United States and it is illegal to manufacture, distribute, or possess Rohypnol in this country.

Some of the common street names are Roofies, Rope, Forget Pill, and Mexican Valium (because you can buy a tablet in Mexico for about forty cents and sell it in the United States for anywhere between two and six dollars). It is generally mailed or smuggled across the border. Several packages seized in Miami in the past years were shipped from Cali, Colombia, and contained up to eleven thousand dosage units each.

The drug usually starts to take effect in about fifteen to twenty minutes and full effect occurs in thirty to sixty minutes and lasts for approximately four to six hours. As a powerful sedative, it may make you look and act like you are drunk; you will slur your words and have trouble standing or walking.

Initially you may feel confused, disoriented, and light-headed. As the drug's effects progress, you will experience a loss of inhibitions, impaired judgment, and reduced levels of consciousness. Eventually you may be rendered unconscious and unable to resist an attack. Some people describe an almost "out-of-body experience" where they were aware of what was going on but could not react or resist.

As with the other date rape drugs, one of the most troubling side effects is that it can cause anterograde amnesia, which is an absence of memory for events that occur after it is ingested. This means that you will not remember whom you were with, what you did, and what was done to you while you were under the influence of the drug. This can cause you to be uncertain about what happened to you, leading to delays or even reluctance to get tested and provide biological samples for toxicology testing.

Depending upon how much has been ingested, the drug's metabolic properties are detectable in urine for up to seventy-two hours after ingestion. The drug looks like aspirin and is colorless and odorless when mixed with a beverage, usually alcohol.

Since February 1999, reformulated Rohypnol tablets, which turn blue in liquid to increase visibility, have been approved and marketed in twenty countries. In response to the new blue tablets, predators serve blue tropical drinks and punches or dark liquids, such as cola, to disguise the blue dye. The original colorless tablets are still available as well.

Though Rohypnol is now the least common club drug, it is still readily available across the southern half of the United States, from Southern California to Florida, reflecting its path from Mexico and Latin America.

When in Doubt, Dump It Out

Karen, a retired police officer with fourteen years' experience in law enforcement, was vacationing in Florida with a girlfriend. They stopped at a popular boating club where they planned to have drinks and then dinner. The place was packed and they had to wait for an empty table in the patio seating area. As they stood, a man seated nearby invited them to take the two empty seats left at his table. He was with three of his friends and they all had mixed drinks. As Karen finished up her first Corona and lime she excused herself to go to the ladies' room and asked her friend to order another round. When she came back, she noticed that the man across from her had switched from a mixed drink to a Corona and lime, but she didn't think anything of it. She hadn't even finished her second beer when she began feeling very strange. Her head was spinning and she felt woozy and nauseous. Something was very wrong. Her friend took her back to the hotel, where Karen vomited and slept for ten hours straight. When she woke up she could not remember returning to the hotel or even throwing up.

Her experience as a police officer told her that there was no doubt she had been drugged, and like a good investigator, she put the pieces together. When she had gotten up to go to the ladies' room and asked her friend to order another round, that clued in one or more of the men at the table that she'd be drinking another Corona and lime. The guy across from her ordered one for himself, too, slipped in a drug (probably GHB), and switched beers when her girlfriend wasn't looking. Karen knew her friend would always look out for her, but she didn't account for a distraction, possibly caused by one of the men at the table, that caused her friend to take her eyes off the newly delivered Corona and lime.

Never leave your drink unattended. All it takes is a second or two for someone to slip something into it and put you into a dangerous position. When you are out, use caution and watch your drink at all times. You might get caught up in a conversation, give hello or goodbye hugs to friends, make phone calls, even do something as basic as turn your head to wave to an acquaintance across the room. Take your drink with you, have it in your hand, or cover it with your hand. If you use the restroom, so does your drink. If you go to the dance floor, your drink goes to the dance floor.

On Guard

If you walk into a bar and a friendly guy greets you by handing you a drink, absolutely do not drink it. If you walk into a party and you are welcomed with a glass of fruit punch or sangria or any other drink by an amicable stranger, do not drink it. Be very suspicious of anyone you don't know who offers you a drink. He may even be someone known to you. You might have friends in common. That does not mean you should trust him. Men, especially sexual predators, know that finding a commonality with a woman will give her a false sense of security. Don't be caught off guard, and instead use the following responses to say "no."

- Thanks, but I just had one.

- No, thank you. I'm just too full to have a drink right now.

- No, thank you. I have to drive my friend home.

- No, thank you. I have to drive myself home.

- No, thank you. I forgot I'm the designated driver.

- No, thank you. I am still recovering from a cold.

- Thanks for the offer, but I'm pacing myself.

- Thank you for the offer, but I'd really rather get my own drink.

If you instinctively happen to take the drink, hold it, take it to the ladies' room, spill it, or put it down and forget about it, but under no circumstances drink it.

Play It Safe: Top 10 Rules

1. Do not accept a drink from anyone you don't know.

2. If someone offers you a drink from the bar at a club or party, watch it being poured. However, be aware that bartenders may work in concert with predators to spike drinks with a date rape drug.

3. Do not drink from a common punch or juice bowl or from any container that is being shared.

4. Be aware that the top of a plastic bottle of water can be opened, contaminated, and resealed or glued to appear to be unopened.

5. Listen for the "fizz" on twist bottles and the sound of a breaking seal.

6. Bring your own drinks to parties.

7. If there is talk of date rape drugs or if your friends seem too drunk for the amount they consumed, leave immediately.

8. If you think something has been slipped into your drink, get to someone you trust, go to the hospital, and take your drink with you.

9. Ask to be tested for date rape drugs as soon as possible. The drugs leave your system rapidly.

10. Trust your intuition. If you feel that something is wrong, that a guy is a creep, then he most likely is.

What to Do if You See Someone Spiking Another Person's Drink

The most important thing you can do if you see someone spiking another person's drink is to take action. By doing so you will likely be averting a dangerous and potentially horrific situation.

You may be reluctant to get involved for a variety of reasons. But think to yourself, "That could be my sister, my cousin, my girlfriend, my daughter, or even me." If it were someone you loved, what would you want the person witnessing the potential beginning of a drug-facilitated sexual assault to do? You would want them to act.

Here is a list of some options you have to get involved. Be specific with what you observed, but remember: if you think you saw someone put something into another person's drink, you saw someone put something into someone's drink. It may be hard to believe that you witnessed something so heinous.

- Tell the bartender, waiter, or waitress.

- Warn the woman before she begins to consume the drink.

- Ask, "Did you just put something in her drink?" (Put the burden on him.)

- If she has left her seat, intercept her before she returns.

- Call the police or 911.

Believe Your Eyes

You may be sitting in a bar, waiting for your friends, mindlessly watching people around you. You may see any of these behaviors:

- A woman gets up to go to the restroom or to the bar—the predator will likely do a scan before he acts. He will reach across the table for the drink, pour the drug in, and then stir it.

- He will pick up the drink, hold it below the table, pour the drug in, and then stir it.

- He may stand up and use his body to shield himself while he pours the drug into the drink.

- He may be working in concert with the bartender or bouncer.

Placing a drug in someone's drink is categorized as an assault in most states and is a serious felony.

What to Do if You Believe Your Drink Has Been Spiked

If you believe that someone has spiked your drink it may:

- Fizz.
- Taste salty.
- Have a ring of sediment around the top of the glass.
- Make you nauseous.
- Have a barely detectable odd taste.

Most date rape drugs are odorless, colorless, and tasteless, but if you believe that you have a drink that has been spiked, you will want to secure it and give it to the police for laboratory analysis. Many date rape drugs will not stay in your system for very long. The half-life for GHB, for example, could be as little as an hour.* Date rape drugs can also be detected through hair analysis. Having possession of a glass that was contaminated by a

---

* A drug's half-life is the time needed for the concentration or amount of the drug in the body to be reduced by one half.

predator will yield a great deal of physical evidence in a drug-facilitated sexual assault (DFSA).

> ### HOW WILL I KNOW IF MY DRINK HAS BEEN SPIKED?
>
> If your drink has been spiked, you may not be able to see, smell, or taste it. The drug or extra alcohol may be colorless and odorless and may not affect the taste of your drink.
> Warning signs include:
> - Feeling dizzy or faint.
> - Feeling ill or sleepy.
> - Feeling drunk even if you think you've only had a little alcohol to drink.
> - Passing out.
> - Waking up feeling uncomfortable and confused, with memory blanks about the night before.

What If

Despite your best intentions, you may wake up with a strange feeling in your gut. Maybe you feel like you had sex with someone, though you are unable to remember if you actually did. Or you recall accepting a drink and then have no memory of what happened afterward. You are confused and unable to account for the evening. Whatever the trigger, intuitively you know something is wrong.

You might not yet know what you will want to do in the long run. For the immediate present, here are steps you can take to preserve evidence as you consider options in the future. Contact a rape crisis center for help and support. One of the first things to do is to get medical care right away. Call 911 or go to a hospital emergency room for a sexual assault examination. Don't shower, bathe, wash your hands, or brush your teeth before you have a medical evaluation. Save the clothing you were wearing and any other materials that might contain evidence of the drug you may have been given (such as the glass with your drink).

Tell the hospital that you think something was slipped into your drink and that you were drugged. They will have a protocol they will follow. They will take blood and urine samples that can be saved for further laboratory testing. In addition, they may take hair samples, also to be used in later tests.

Date Rape Drug Detectors

You will find coasters, nail polish, and other devices that claim they can detect date rape drugs in your drink. As of this writing, there is a lack of reliable data on whether these tests actually work. You should not bet your safety on them. They may seem like a shield, but they would be a very weak shield and it is far better to rely on good decision making and common sense. In addition, you can test your drink but a date rape drug could still be added to it later.

Bouncers and Bartenders Are Not Always Your Friends

Don't trust the bartender or bouncer to watch your drink. First, it is not part of their job description. The bartender's job is to make drinks, not keep a watchful eye on yours or look out for troublemakers. More important, though, there are many cases in which the bartender or the bouncer acts as a predator. Their job in a bar or club gives them a position from which they can identify and select women who seem vulnerable: the women who are alone or drunk or are simply not watching their drink. On occasion, the bartender and bouncer have acted in concert or with a third-party predator to take advantage of soft targets.

Ecstasy (MDMA)

Ecstasy is a hallucinogenic and stimulant drug made from the chemical methylenedioxymethamphetamine, otherwise known as MDMA. Recently a form of ecstasy has begun appearing by the name Molly. The use of Molly is becoming more popular under the false belief that it is purer and therefore has fewer negative side effects than ecstasy. There is no quality control over the actual content of these illegal drugs, so it's difficult to say which poison is the lesser, but most believe that Molly is a new name for an old drug that can have deadly consequences. It is available in powder and pill form.

Ecstasy is popular in the club and party scene. In some cases, ecstasy can be used to assist in sexual assault. When slipped into a drink, it is tasteless and presents no immediate warning signs. Once ingested, the drug can last in your system for four to six hours. It can stay in the body for two to five days, which allows a larger window of time for testing if necessary.

MDMA causes changes in perception, including euphoria and increased sensitivity to touch, energy, sensual and sexual arousal, the need to be touched, and the need for stimulation. Some unwanted psychological effects: confusion, anxiety, depression, paranoia, sleep problems, and drug craving.

In high doses, MDMA can interfere with the body's ability to regulate temperature. On occasion, this can lead to a sharp increase in body temperature (hyperthermia), resulting in liver, kidney, and cardiovascular system failure and death.

Although MDMA is known among users as ecstasy, researchers have determined that many tablets contain not only MDMA but also a number of other drugs or drug combinations that can be harmful, such as methamphetamine, ketamine, cocaine, the over-the-counter cough suppressant dextromethorphan (DXM), the diet drug ephedrine, and caffeine.

Spice/K2

K2 and Spice are just two of the many trade names or brands for synthetic designer drugs that are intended to mimic THC, the main active ingredient of marijuana. These designer synthetic drugs are from the synthetic cannabinoid class of drugs that are often marketed and sold under the guise of "herbal incense" or "potpourri."

As research by the Drug Enforcement Administration (DEA) has shown, inside the brightly colored packaging are wildly unpredictable and often dangerous chemical compounds created in laboratories. Since 2009, law enforcement has encountered approximately ninety-five different synthetic cannabinoids that are being sold as "legal" alternatives to marijuana. These products are abused for their psychoactive properties and are packaged without information as to their health and safety risks.

Synthetic cannabinoids are sold under names like K2 and Spice, as well as many other names, at small convenience stores, head shops, gas stations, and via the Internet from both domestic and international sources. These products are labeled "not for human consumption" in an attempt to shield the manufacturers, distributors, and retail sellers from criminal prosecution. This type of marketing is nothing more than a means to make dangerous psychoactive substances widely available to the public.

How K2/Spice Affects the Mind

Acute psychotic episodes are associated with use of these synthetic cannabinoids. Some individuals have suffered intense hallucinations. Other effects from smoking products laced with these substances include severe agitation, disorganized thoughts, paranoid delusions, and violence. These drugs could cause a woman to become incapacitated to the point of being defenseless.

The most important fact to understand about synthetic marijuana is that it isn't just one substance. It is a family of man-made chemicals.

Synthetic marijuana should in no way be confused with its organic namesake, and there is no way to know what chemical combination you are allowing into your body. In the summer of 2016, over a three-day period in New York City, 130 people were treated in hospital emergency rooms for K2/Spice overdoses.

Other street names include Blaze, Paradise, Dream, Spike, and Mr. Nice Guy.

Don't Let the "Ladies Only" Sign Fool You

Isabel (not her real name), a young nurse, was out dancing with friends at Social Bar, a three-story nightclub on Manhattan's West Side. At about 2 a.m., a thirty-year-old construction worker from Pennsylvania approached and tried to join her on the dance floor. Turning her back toward him, she shrugged off his attempts and kept dancing with her friends. Completely understandable and normal behavior when you are having fun with a group of people you know and want to avoid interacting with a man you don't know, especially at two in the morning.

She was not aware of a group of guys nearby who witnessed his public rejection and who even made a few mocking comments. Fueled by a toxic mixture of alcohol, embarrassment, and rage, he was infuriated and began stalking her.

She left her group to make a trip to the ladies' room, alone, at 2:30 a.m. It was the chance he was waiting for. He followed her in, pushed open the door of the stall, and beat her with his fists. She was left unconscious on the bathroom floor with a broken nose, a broken eye socket, a broken jaw, a fractured skull, and a wound on her head that required fifty stiches. She may have also been sexually abused.

The construction worker was seen on surveillance video leaving the club, shaking his hand as though it was injured. At a nearby bodega he was also captured on video stealing a can of beer. He ended up pleading guilty to assault and attempted sexual assault and was sentenced to sixteen years in prison.

The Uneven Playing Field

As I mention in the introduction to this book, crimes against women are different from those against men because of what is at stake. Women have to contend with the risk of sexual violence. In addition, a man's public shame and embarrassment is so pervasive and key to understanding his behavior that I always include it in the women's safety and self-defense classes that I teach. A woman may do something she feels is insignificant or even meaningless, such as rejecting someone on the dance floor, yet it can induce an extreme response. Understanding the humiliation factor will help you stay safe.

In the case of Isabel, her actions were inconsequential and unimportant to her. A stranger approached her and she turned him away. Happens all the time in clubs. Yet for the worker, it caused feelings of failure and weakness, leading to a vicious attack. This is not in any way an excuse for such barbaric behavior, but it happens.

When you are out in a social situation, try to maintain a degree of awareness with regard to your interactions with men, especially those you don't know or whom you have turned down. You can move into the orange zone and monitor them.

Ideally, the concept of going out as a group and going home as a group will be extended when you are inside a club or at a party. If you have to use the ladies' room, go with at least one other person. Predators have two fears: getting caught and getting hurt. Both those fears are compounded when they have to face a second person, and it is usually not a scenario they want.

A Closer Look: Go Out as a Group, Go Home as a Group

Sticking to the *go out as a group, go home as a group* rule and picking a designated mom are solid ways to be safe during an evening out. In any social setting, where there are people you don't know and alcohol is being consumed, it pays to be aware and alert. However, when you are with a group, it can be challenging to make sure everyone stays together, especially when drinking is involved.

▶ *What if you're with the group, everyone around you is getting sloppy drunk, and you just want to go home?*

You go home. A toxic environment will probably become rowdier and more dangerous for you as the night goes on. At the start of the evening, figure out in advance a couple of ways to get home in case your original plan falls through. Keep in mind that if you have been drinking, your decision making will likely be diminished, so having an alternative arrangement is a positive, proactive move.

Whenever you go out, always do the following:

- Bring cash.
- Have your identification.
- Bring your cell phone.
- Call a cab, Uber, or Lyft rather than hailing one on the street.
- Beware of the fake-taxi scam, where a woman is picked up after hailing what she believes is a real taxi and is then robbed or worse.
- If you're traveling, take a hotel business card or snap a photo with your cell phone.

▶ *After a fun night out, you and your friends agree to meet by the front door and leave in fifteen minutes. You get there a little later—bathroom line—and realize they've left without you. What do you do?*

This can easily happen, especially at a large party or in a loud club. You miscommunicate, lose each other, or get stuck waiting for the bathroom.

As in the case above, having a backup plan in place to get home or to your dorm or anywhere safe before you go out is always a smart idea. And again, carry cash, your cell phone, and a photo ID at all times.

▶ *You are the designated mom for the night, the group is ready to leave, and one of your friends wants to stay behind and talk to a guy she met. What should you do?*

While you know it's best to stick with the original plan and go home as a group, you'll frequently have situations where someone wants to break away. If she has her wits about her and is not in a condition that would compromise her safety, you may have no choice. You'll only frustrate the both of you if you insist that she go home. If she's in no condition to make good decisions, you may have to take matters into your own hands and be convincingly persistent. A decent guy may try to help persuade her to go with you. If he happens not to be so decent, it's even more important to remove her.

> **Answers to the sexual predator quiz:**
> All false. You never know who is a potential sexual predator.

TAKEAWAYS

- Go out as a group, go home as a group.
- Have a designated "mom" for the night.
- Date rape drugs are colorless, odorless, and tasteless. They will leave you incapacitated, unable to defend yourself from sexual assault. You also might not clearly remember what happened.
- Always watch your drink; when in doubt, dump it out.
- Bring cash, your cell phone, and a photo ID.
- Make a backup plan, or two, for how to get home.
- Bartenders and bouncers are not your friends.
- Be aware of the humiliation factor when interacting with men in a social situation.

6

HAVE A BLUEPRINT: THE ULTIMATE SELF-DEFENSE WEAPON

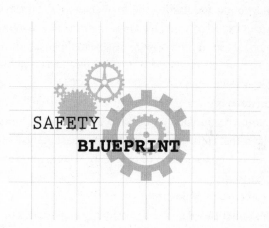

SAFETY
BLUEPRINT

W hat is the most powerful weapon in your body? Your brain. It is
hardwired to protect you by using intuition. Almost instantaneously, it analyzes the actions and behavior of people around
you and sends out danger alerts. With a little effort, you can make your
mind even more powerful and adept at keeping you safe. You won't have
to go running or to the gym. You will need to do mental exercises and
visualize "what-if" scenarios to create blueprints, or action plans, that will
be ready to be employed when the time or need arises. Visualization is used
in law enforcement to help officers be prepared for all kinds of situations

on the street. Similarly, in the military, where it is referred to as emergence conditioning, it is used to get soldiers ready for action in the field.

By imagining scenarios involving crime and violence and picturing what you would do in response, you are creating a mental map to help you when someone intends to harm you or your family. Your ability to make decisions under threat will be enhanced and your self-defense options, including avoidance, escape, and de-escalation, will also be increased through the process.

Imagine your brain as a filing cabinet, organizing and storing facts, knowledge, and information. Everything you have read, learned, or thought about has a place. Some folders are thick, used frequently, while others are filed away, to be referred to later. For most people, the file labeled SELF-DEFENSE is thin. You may hear about an incident and spend a second wondering what you would do in that situation, but then you let it go. It is scary to think about, and finding the correct answer seems daunting. But when you are unexpectedly involved in something like road rage, stalking, home invasion, or assault, you want to be able to flip instantly in your brain to a well-informed self-defense file. If it's empty when you need it most, you are left as a soft target.

The good news is that through visualization, you will become familiar with the unknown and you can develop an unlimited number of blueprints, or plans, that can guide you on how to react in most any situation. Moreover, you can go back and continuously expand upon and refine the details of your plans.

Unless you have previous training, instinctively knowing what to do when you are under threat and in a potentially dangerous situation is very difficult, almost impossible. The flight-fight-freeze response kicks in when you are scared. Initially your body will experience a surge of chemicals, particularly adrenaline, giving you a burst of energy. Your resting heart rate of about 60 to 80 beats per minute can quickly escalate to as high as 170 to 200 beats per minute. Your blood pressure will increase and you will breathe more rapidly. You will possibly get tunnel vision, fixing your vision only on an object in front of you, and experience auditory exclusion. It will be difficult to focus and even harder to think rationally. With the blueprint in place, your subconscious mind will be able to access it and you will automatically go through steps that can assist you. Importantly, a blueprint will help control your adrenal response so that you don't immediately freeze when faced with overwhelming odds.

I have firsthand experience with the power of having a mental blueprint. As a result of visualization, at age seventeen, I saved the life of an eight-year-old boy. Early that summer, the recreation department of my hometown mailed out a flyer listing upcoming events for the season. Included in the envelope was a pamphlet describing mouth-to-mouth resuscitation and CPR. Fascinated, I studied it intently.

In July, as I was walking on a broad, virtually deserted beach, I saw a young woman jerk out of a beach chair and start frantically waving her arms for help. Running over, I spotted two feet, barely sticking out of a sand dune. A boy. Digging as fast as I could, I grabbed him under his arms and lifted him out of the sand. He wasn't breathing and his eyes were full of blood. By this point, about twenty adults had gathered, standing in shock. Looking around, I asked if anyone knew how to do mouth-to-mouth resuscitation. To my dismay, everyone stared, paralyzed. My heart raced. I fought off panic.

Everything I had read in that pamphlet came rushing back to me. I automatically reacted, pinching his nose and blowing into his mouth. I performed rescue breathing for about two minutes, until he started taking in air on his own. According to the doctors, another minute without air and he would have been dead. The good-news story was even picked up by the Associated Press and distributed nationwide. See how a blueprint, even if you've only reviewed it once, can make a difference?

In this chapter you will read about a variety of situations, ranging from panhandlers to robbery to active shooters, and the basic steps to take if you find yourself in one of them. Visualizing plans and actions, even one time, will give you tools for how to react. The self-defense file will no longer be empty.

Thinking about violence and imagining it happening to you can be uncomfortable and disturbing. Luckily, creating a useful blueprint is a quick process. You can spend one minute or less thinking about what-if scenarios and reviewing the steps you would take. Over time, you can reassess, add details, and expand your original blueprint.

You can do this on the go, when something jogs your memory. For example, you may be leaving the mall and think to yourself, "What would

I have done if someone had approached me in that empty parking lot?" Maybe you are on the subway and someone is hustling for money. Ask yourself, "What would I do if he asked me, I said no, and he kept at it?" Alternatively, when you are safe at home and can delve deeper into your thought process, you might spend extra time mentally going through your actions. Imagine this as a series of brief episodes on how you can be safer.

The steps I suggest below cover the fundamentals. It is impossible to account for all possible variations of crime, so basic outlines are presented. You can further empower yourself and think up responses and plans on your own, or review the ones in this book and go into more detail. When you hear about a crime in the news or learn that something has happened to family or friends or someone in your community, stop and think about what you would do if it happened to you. Over time, you will create a mental file full of blueprints that your brain can access if need be.

As you create blueprints through the process of visualization, keep the following in mind:

■ Envision yourself going through the steps in each scenario in as much vivid detail as possible. Over time, add complications where you have to problem-solve. For example, you are rushing to work and quickly change lanes without using your blinker. The man in the car behind you is enraged and starts honking, pulling up next to you, making obscene gestures. You try de-escalation, mouthing "I'm sorry" and waving your hand, but it doesn't work. What do you do next? (The answer is you drive to a place where there are people, whether it is a gas station or convenience store or local police station, stay in your car, and honk the horn for help.)

■ Don't be discouraged if the first few times you feel uncomfortable. Expect to experience a minor adrenaline surge during the initial visualizations. Your heart rate will likely increase. Remember, these are what-if scenarios and you only need to spend a short amount of time reviewing them.

■ A predator wants isolation and control. The purpose of the blueprint is to thwart his plans.

■ Always see yourself coming out successful and winning. You need to believe that you can and will prevail. It's the only option.

Below, I walk you through a sample visualization to create a blueprint to deal with someone breaking into the place where you live. Reviewing it the first time will be the hardest; after that it will get easier. You might be able to go into more detail with subsequent run-throughs, such as realizing you want to keep an extra phone charger in your safe room. Or you may hear about a similar break-in in the news. In that instance, the family kept a discreet nanny cam pointed at their door and police were able to make an arrest based on that video footage. Now you might decide to also set up a nanny cam in a similar location.

A visualization goes like this:

Imagine that you are in your apartment/dorm room/house. The doorknob rattles repeatedly. It sounds like someone is trying to break in. What do you do? Visualize the following steps to create a blueprint for this scenario.

1. Grab your cell phone.

2. Run to your safe room. It can be the bathroom or even a closet. (Later in this chapter I cover the importance of a safe room and how to set one up.)

3. Lock the door. Put the safety bar under the doorknob.

4. Dial the local police department. You should have your police department phone number for where you live and where you work entered into your favorites so that you can call them directly, by pressing one button. When you are stressed and your heart rate reaches 115 beats per minute, you begin to lose your fine motor skills, which include the ability to press the buttons on the phone. Moreover, if you dial 911 you may reach a regional answering center that may be far from your actual location. (If you use a landline, your exact location will be provided to the dispatcher.)

5. Practice repeating out loud, "I live at *123 Main St., Anywhere, USA,* and someone is trying to break into my home. Please send help." Be prepared to provide a cross street or landmark to decrease response time.

You have done all you can. Now you rely on the dispatcher and the police to give you instructions on what to do next.

Panhandlers and Scammers

Ambush in the Mall

Panhandlers and scammers are similar to aggressive salespeople. They all want something from you and will use intrusive tactics, purposefully not giving you time to pause, to get what they want.

Shopping malls frequently have small kiosks selling everything from body lotion to earrings to cell phones. You may scurry past, avoiding eye contact, but are greeted with a warm hello, followed up by "Would you like to try . . . ?"

It doesn't matter what it is. If you stop to try whatever they are selling, you are likely to hand over a few dollars for something you didn't intend to buy. Envision yourself walking through the mall and being solicited by the salesperson. When you hear the words "Excuse me, would you like to try . . . ?" see yourself not responding and continuing on your way. Remember that the salesperson is not reaching out to you out of kindness or because they are being nice. By the same token, you are not being rude by paying no attention to them. Their goal is to engage with you to persuade you to buy something you had no intention of purchasing.

This same concept also applies to a predator, except that the stakes are now much higher because of the involvement of a criminal element. The more time you spend in close confines and engaged in any way with a predator, in this case a panhandler or swindler, the more likely your safety is to be compromised. A common tactic used by a salesperson and a predator is to ask you a question to get you to interact with them. They are both sizing you up: the salesperson to get you to buy something and the predator to see how soft a target you are.

As you walk by a kiosk, a salesperson calls out, "Can I ask you a question?" Your curiosity is piqued and you stop and engage with him. A predator may ask you for the time. You pull out your cell to look and in a second he swipes the phone, and then he and the cell are gone.

Create a Blueprint

1. See yourself walking and being approached by a stranger who asks a question. It doesn't matter what the question is.

2. In vivid detail and without missing a step, say, "Sorry, I don't," or, "No thank you."

3. Don't stop walking, keep moving.

Checkout Charity

Much as a criminal relies on the element of surprise, large corporate entities that solicit money from you at the checkout counter rely on the same principle. You are standing in line, with ten people behind you. You get to the cashier and are asked to contribute to a cause. It's called checkout charity and is a way for organizations to get a little bit of money from a lot of people. You are caught off guard—you don't have time to research the cause and you don't want to look like a cheapskate—so you hand over a few dollars to the cashier. You walk out of the store feeling like you have been scammed.

Create a Blueprint

1. See yourself going through checkout.

2. When the cashier hits you up, say, "Thank you, but I already gave."

The same practice can be applied to panhandlers, with a slight modification:

1. See yourself being asked for money.

2. Say, "Sorry, I don't carry cash," as you continue walking away.

Catcalling

An exception to the rule of not walking around with headphones is wearing them in midday, with no music playing, as a way to discourage interaction with aggressive men. In this case, you pretend to listen to music so that they will assume you have not heard them if they shout obscenities or try to start a conversation. You are also denying them what they seek, which is your reaction and attention. This type of behavior can be engaged in by a lone man but most often it is in the presence of other men.

Road Rage

Most of us don't consider ourselves to be the cause of road rage, but if you are an aggressive or careless driver, then you might be triggering an extreme reaction in another motorist. The end result can be violence and, in some cases, fatalities. The aggression can escalate until one driver runs the other off the road, or worse.

Treat other drivers with the same consideration that you would use if you were on foot in a public space. When you are not careful with your driving, it can be perceived as combative or threatening, similar to walking in a crowd and elbowing people around you to push through. Aggressive driving is a traffic offense and acts of road rage are often criminal in nature. While you can't control the actions of other drivers, you do have choices in how you drive and how you respond to someone else's aggressive driving.

Take this short quiz to see if you may be the cause of road rage. Answer honestly!

1. Do you regularly drive over the speed limit or accelerate when the traffic light turns yellow?
2. Do you tailgate or flash your headlights when the driver in front of you is driving too slow?
3. Do you honk your horn often?
4. Do you use obscene gestures or communicate angrily at other drivers?

If you answered yes to any of these questions, you may be the cause of road rage in other people.

If you answered no to all of them, consider these additional triggers that can cause road rage:

- Not using your turn signal
- Abrupt lane changes
- Failure to dim high beams
- Distracted driving using phone or putting on makeup
- Driving slowly in passing lane

Simply adhering to the rules of the road reduces your chances of being involved in a road rage incident.

Additionally, take these steps to avoid being the target of an irate driver:

PLAN AHEAD: Leave yourself plenty of time to get to your destination.

DE-ESCALATE: A simple hand wave and mouthing "Sorry!" can defuse most situations.

Take a Deep Breath

If you're on the receiving end of an aggressive driver, take a breath before you do anything. Ask yourself, "Is it worth possibly ruining my day, or worse?"

Hostility Is Toxic

Hostility is not only unhealthy, but it also leads to even more hostility. Acting aggressively against a belligerent driver ups the ante. Let it go. You will be glad you did, and if you don't, you may wish you had.

Fake Police Pull-Over

The flashing red and blue lights on the front grille of a truck caught Tammy, an off-duty police sergeant, off guard. Still in uniform, she was driving home after a long day. At first, she thought it was an unmarked police car, and her initial reaction was "What was I doing wrong to get pulled over?"

Quickly she realized, however, that something was not right. She wasn't speeding, she was on her home turf just north of Houston, and she didn't recognize the vehicle that pulled her over. The truck with the lights slowed to a stop beside her. The driver must have seen her uniform because he immediately hit the gas and took off. She followed him and called for backup. Eventually the twenty-one-year-old driver was caught and arrested for impersonating a police officer, considered a felony in Texas and in most other states.

Being pulled over can be a traumatic experience, especially for the first time. The sight of multicolored lights flashing behind you, a bright beam shining onto your vehicle, and an officer in uniform appearing at your car door are disconcerting. Moreover, you will assume you are being stopped because you committed some type of traffic violation—in other words, because you broke the law. That is scary. If you find yourself wondering whether it really is an officer, or if it is someone impersonating one, then getting pulled over quickly becomes an unnerving and intimidating ordeal.

If you are being pulled over by a uniformed officer, in a marked car, with roof and grille lights and flashing headlights, it is very unlikely that it is a fake pull-over. Years ago, a police car was usually a Ford Crown Victoria, a Chevy Impala, or a Chevy Lumina, but today it can be any one of a variety of subcompacts to full-size Ford F-150s. Included in this list are Chevy Corvettes, Ford Mustangs, Chevy Camaros, and other high-performance cars or trucks.

An unmarked police car usually won't have reflecting tape or roof lights and will utilize more supplementary lights to draw your attention. There may be dash lights, side mirror lights, and flashing turn-signal lights. Some police officers take their cars home and use them while off-duty or on call and will not always be in uniform when they pull you over.

An officer in uniform should put you at ease even though it is possible to purchase security guard uniforms that look almost the same as those a police officer wears. If you are in any doubt, call 911 and give the operator a detailed location of where you are and descriptions of your vehicle and the police vehicle. The 911 dispatcher will be able to use that information to check with the local police or sheriff's department to confirm that it is an actual police vehicle and that the officer is legitimate.

A real police officer in civilian clothing will approach your car with his ID in hand. He will have a badge and an ID card that provide his name, rank, the police department he works for, and his corresponding badge number. He should allow you ample time to examine his credentials. If he only flashes his badge or he refuses to show you his ID, keep your doors locked and only open your window a few inches. If someone produces a police department business card, it is not proof of any authority. Police department business cards have been used in the past by criminals posing as police officers. Assessing his demeanor may also give you a clue: Does he have presence and is he calm and confident? Keep in mind that new, or rookie, officers may act and present themselves as unsure.

A good way to gauge whether it is a real pull-over is to determine whether you've broken any laws. Some traffic laws may vary from state to state, but here are a few basic ones that can cause you to be pulled over:

- Exceeding the posted speed limit by five or more miles per hour.

- Changing lanes without signaling, making an illegal U-turn, crossing a double yellow line, or swerving and driving erratically.

- Driving at night or in inclement weather (in some states) without your headlights, or if you have a burned-out bulb in your head-lights, taillights, or turn signals.

If you haven't done anything wrong and a vehicle is attempting to pull you over, especially at night and/or in a remote area, you should be cautious and keep your guard up. Most law enforcement agencies understand that drivers may not want to pull over on highways that are unlit and that there may be many miles between exits. The worst thing that could come out of not stopping in a timely manner is likely to be a ticket for failing to comply with the police.

However, if you are doing something reckless, like driving 90 miles per hour or creating a danger to the public, you might be pulled over by an unmarked car with an officer in civilian clothing. Under these circumstances, the officer may not be very patient with you.

Attitudes and reactions vary from police officer to police officer. Be sincere. You don't want to give the police officer the impression that you are playing games.

What to Expect if You Are Pulled Over by the Police

An officer never knows what to expect when he pulls someone over. He has his safety and the safety of the public in mind, so don't be put off by his professional or stern approach.

When you are pulled over for a violation, it is likely that the officer will first ask you for your license and registration. He will then tell you the reason for stopping you. The officer has several options: he can write you a ticket, give you a written warning (not in all states), or give you a verbal warning. It's likely that what you say and your attitude will contribute to his decision on what action to take. His goal is to deter you from committing the same violation again. If he thinks you understand what you did and that you are not likely to commit the same violation again, at least not in the near future, he can elect to give you a verbal or written warning. If he feels that a ticket is in order, then he will issue you one.

When you realize you are being asked to pull over, take the following steps:

1. Switch on your four-way hazard lights.

2. Slow down to a reasonably low speed, just enough to let the officer know that you're not trying to flee and that you acknowledge that you are being pulled over.

3. Turn on the dome light inside your vehicle so the officer can see you clearly and know that you're not reaching for a weapon or attempting to conceal contraband.

4. Keep your hands where the officer can see them and avoid any sudden or unnecessary movements.

5. Wait for the officer to ask you for your driver's license and registration before you retrieve them. He will watch you closely when you look into your purse, glove compartment, or console. He's not being nosy, he's being cautious.

6. As with any interaction, be sincere and polite. The officer wants to go home to his family at the end of his shift.

I do not recommend trying to be funny or sarcastic or trying to talk your way out of a ticket. If the officer intends to issue you a ticket, take it and don't try to debate it on the side of the road. That is what the courtroom is for. Your attitude will be noted in the officer's notes. Many busy courts will offer you a reduced plea with the officer's approval. Lastly, understand that some areas and traffic details are zero tolerance and the officer has no discretion on whether or not you receive a summons.

Carjacking

In 2013, a thirty-year-old lawyer and his wife were shopping at an upscale mall in Short Hills, New Jersey. The couple had just returned to their car after picking up Christmas presents when they were approached by two men who wanted their late-model Range Rover. When the husband resisted, he was shot and killed. The thieves fled in the car and four men were later arrested.

Carjacking is a robbery in which a motor vehicle is taken directly from the driver and occurs most often in a busy commercial area, when the owner is getting in or out of the car. Most (65 percent) carjackings or carjacking attempts occur within five miles of the owner's home and on weekends. Carjackers tend to rob lone drivers more often (92 percent), for obvious reasons. More than 90 percent of carjackings occur in cities or suburbs. They usually take place between 7 p.m. and midnight.

Anytime you stop, for whatever reason, you are a potential target. This includes stopping at traffic lights and stop signs, and places with a high level of turnover such as gas stations, rest areas, and fast-food drive-thrus. Car-bump lures, staging fake accidents, and being followed home from a shopping center are also common occurrences. While not as frequent as during the 1990s and 2000s, they are still a major concern and thousands occur each year.

Always be aware of your surroundings, especially when you are entering or exiting your car. Keep your doors locked at all times and roll up the windows when you are going to a location where you will be slowing down or parking. If you are approached by someone when you are getting in or out of your car, throw your keys at them and run.

Create a Blueprint

1. Visualize exiting a mall or shopping center and having one or two men suddenly appear at your side. Intuitively, you know they are bad people.

2. In vivid detail, hear them saying, "Give me your keys or I'll kill you."

3. Envision a gun being pointed at you. This is a business transaction: your property for your life. Don't gamble it away.

4. See yourself tossing the predator your keys as you move away, leaving your belongings behind. Often in a situation like this, you will only remember seeing the barrel of a gun. If you have created your blueprint, you are more likely to have less tunnel vision and will

remember more details. It will help later to give a good description of the criminal(s).

5. Run back to the mall or wherever there are people.

Dangers at the Pump

Returning to school from a visit home, a twenty-three-year-old Binghamton University student was pumping gas at a Pennsylvania service station when a man jumped into her driver's seat. When she climbed into the passenger seat to rescue her two cats, he pulled her in and sped off, her legs hanging out of the car. He struck her and announced he had a gun and was fleeing to Virginia. After a 150-mile ride, which ended when he was forced to stop for gas, she was able to jump out of the car and run to people for help.

Headlines like "The Fear of Filling Up" and "Do You Need a Bodyguard to Fill Up Your Car" confirm what you may have wondered about. Increasingly, more and more gas stations are becoming danger zones. Assault, robbery, carjacking, thefts, and even murders are occurring at the pump.

Sliders

When you are getting gas, always be on the lookout for "sliders." Thieves stealthily approach the passenger side of your car while you are pumping or paying for gas. They know that women typically leave their purses on the front seat and it is common for drivers to leave the keys in the ignition and the doors unlocked. It is easy to be distracted when filling up. You need to have your credit card handy, select credit or debit, enter your zip code, choose if you would like a receipt, select your grade of gas, and then, finally, begin pumping. Before you have even entered your zip code, thieves have opened your passenger door and made off with your purse.

If a thief approaches you for your car keys, toss them at his chest and run toward the service station. This will greatly reduce your chances of being kidnapped.

Create a Blueprint

1. Envision yourself pulling into a gas station and next to a pump.
2. As you turn off the car, remove your keys from the ignition, lock the doors, and hit the alarm button.

3. Don't leave your purse or anything of value on the front seat; put it on the floor or on the back seat.

4. In addition to your car keys, your credit card is the only thing you need on you when you pump gas.

Car Trouble

The AAA reports that problems with batteries, tires, and keys are the most common reasons members call the AAA for assistance. However, every year there are more than 12 million calls related to engine trouble, fuel issues, and other mechanical problems. It's hard to plan for car trouble, but you can save time and money by investing in routine maintenance to minimize a breakdown, which can lead to something potentially worse. Much like an injured animal, a stalled or broken car on the side of the road can make you become an instant soft target.

What to Do If You Experience Car Trouble

1. Pull off the road in a safe location and activate your emergency flashers.

2. Call 911 with your cell phone.

3. Stay in the car with the windows up and doors locked until official assistance arrives.

4. If you feel it is safe, place an emergency reflector (it's a good idea to have one in your car emergency kit) ten to twenty feet behind your car and get back in until help arrives.

Car Emergency Kit

Always keep an emergency kit in your car. You will not appreciate it until you need it. It should contain the following:

- An emergency flashlight (there are a number of inexpensive, hand-cranking flashlights that do not require batteries)
- A reflector
- Jumper cables

- First-aid kit
- Multipurpose tool such as a Leatherman
- Emergency blanket
- Poncho
- Water
- Fire extinguisher

A fire extinguisher is not only for your safety. If you come upon a car accident in which the driver is trapped inside the vehicle, you could use your extinguisher to break the window or to put out an engine fire.

Road Trip

If you are going on an extended drive, always start out with a full tank of gas, check the spare tire, and make sure your car is in good shape. Never leave keys in the ignition, not even to zip out to run an errand or make a quick stop at a convenience store. Plan your fuel stops and map out well-traveled rest areas where you know you can get the necessities you may need. Get into the practice of filling up when you have a quarter of a tank left. If you're driving on a trip that will require an overnight stay, pick two hotels, one just short of your intended stop and one fifty to seventy-five miles beyond, in the event you feel that you can travel farther. Use travel guides and websites to plan out your stops in advance.

A Car Escape Tool Is a Must

A car escape tool can save your life. Every year, thousands of drivers are trapped in their cars in collisions or from being submerged in water. An escape tool should be able to cut a seat belt, deflate an airbag, or bust out a side window. In an accident, a seat belt can become stuck and you won't be able to release it, your door might not open, or your airbag might be inflated and you will not be able to move.

The tool should be kept somewhere secure. Remember, when you're involved in an accident, everything in your car will be shifted and thrown around (that includes your cell phone). Key-chain emergency tools are likely to be the most secure and you will be able to get to them quickly.

You can also use the tool if you happen upon an accident and the person is trapped and they need to get out of the car immediately.

Create a Blueprint

1. Envision being in a collision, with the airbag pressed against you, rendering you immobile.

2. You smell gas and see that the engine is on fire.

3. You are able to reach your car keys and the escape tool. Use the escape tool to cut your seat belt off, if stuck, and break the window if the door is jammed.

4. The escape tool can also deflate an airbag. Open the car door and run from the vehicle.

What to Do if You're Being Followed

You can check whether you really are being followed by making a series of turns. Circle the block if you are traveling on local roads and, if you are on the highway, exit and get back on. If someone makes the same maneuvers as you have, it's a sure bet something is not right.

The first thing you want to do is slow down and use your cell phone to call 911. Take note of where you are and what direction you are traveling in because those are the first questions the police will ask. It will be extremely helpful to have a cross street or a reference point. They will also want to know the license plate, make, model, and color of your car as well as that of the one following you. And a description of the driver, if possible. Once the police have this information, they will advise you what to do. Do not stop your car and do not engage the driver following you.

You can also drive to the nearest service station, strip mall, or police station. The safest thing to do is to stay in the car and honk the horn for help. If it is late at night, the doors to an establishment may be locked and you do not want to be outside your car if you are being followed. You want to keep a barrier, in this case the car doors, between yourself and the predator. Frequently, these places have surveillance cameras and a predator will be more likely to keep away.

Groping on Public Transportation

■■

Groping on public transportation is a crime promoted by the anonymity of a crowded subway car or bus or platform, where everybody avoids eye contact, and where the predator can make a quick escape at the next stop or disappear behind a pillar or up an escalator.

Major cities in more than fifteen countries have segregation by gender on public transportation. These include Brazil, Mexico, Japan, Indonesia, Pakistan, Thailand, and the United Arab Emirates. Subway cars for women only can be found in Brazil, Egypt, Iran, Japan, Malaysia, Mexico, Nepal, and Russia. Unfortunately, sexually segregated subways and buses don't deter such harassment on subway platforms, bus stops, and on the street.

In New York City, transit workers and nearly all city employees other than law enforcement are forbidden to physically assist people who are in distress or being attacked. So while they can contact police, you shouldn't look for them to be your savior in an assault.

When you get on a subway or are on public transportation, be in the yellow zone and take in the people around you. If you get a strange feeling about someone, pay attention and move to another location. This might not be possible once you are in a crowded bus or train. In that case, hold your purse, coat, or backpack to shield your body to create a barrier.

In addition, no matter how crowded the space, you can still angle your body so that the person is at your left or right and not in front or in back of you. Bring both of your hands up to the bottom of your sternum. If he's on your left side, your left hand will make a fist, and your right hand will go over or cup your left fist so that you can slowly drive the tip of your left elbow into his sternum/stomach area, causing distance between you and him.

It is common to be unsure whether you have been groped. A quick swipe of the hand in a crowded location can be accidental. By the time you conclude that you were, the predator may be gone.

Verbal De-escalation

When you realize someone is groping you, you can verbally confront them and even take their picture or record them on your cell phone. Do not feel embarrassed to cause a scene. Understand that once you protest loudly, others will break out their cell phones and the predator knows it.

Use the following phrases to stop someone and put everyone else on notice that he's up to no good:

- Did you just grope me?
- Don't touch me.
- Stop touching/groping me.
- Back off!

Create a Blueprint

1. See yourself on a crowded subway/bus/train, filled with commuters.

2. Envision that you are being groped and that you have decided to give a verbal response.

3. Be vivid and feel the anger you would feel if someone were violating you.

4. Mouth your response out loud several times in private.

Parking Lot Safety

Most mall-related crimes occur in the parking lots. Drivers and shoppers walking through are vulnerable to being hit by cars, or to falling prey to theft and, in some cases, attacks.

You are heading out for a long-overdue shopping trip and you are excited to get going. It doesn't matter where you are, a big city or a small suburb: if you drop your guard low enough, there will be someone willing to take advantage of you.

Take the following precautions to stay safe:

- When you get to the parking lot, not only are you scanning for a parking space but you're also scanning for anything or anyone that looks out of place.

- Locate a parking spot as close to the front of the store as possible. If you are in a parking structure, park as close to the elevators as possible.

- Avoid anything that will block your view of the store entrance.

- Avoid anything that will block your view when returning to your car. This includes large vehicles, shrubbery, and small structures.

- When you locate a suitable spot, back your car in. Most police officers back their cars in for several reasons: you are able to see obstructions (backing into a parking spot is less dangerous than backing out into traffic) and it provides a quick exit and better visibility when leaving.

- Just before you exit your car, pause and do a quick scan and check your six (behind you).

- As you walk toward the store entrance, do not talk on your cell or text and no using earbuds. Continue to scan as you go.

- As you return to your car, keep your head on a swivel and scan. Once you reach your car, get in immediately and lock the doors.

If you are approached by someone with a question, don't stop, keep walking. Here are some easy responses to memorize in case someone comes near:

- If you're asked to help with car trouble: "Sorry, I don't know anything about cars."
- If you're asked to help with a heavy package: "Sorry, I have a bad back."
- If you're asked for directions: "Sorry, I'm not from around here."
- If you're asked for the time: "I don't have it." Whatever you do, do not stop and look down at your cell phone, even if it is in your hand. You may get punched in the face. It is a common tactic for a predator to smash your face, grab the cell, and run.

Abduction

A young Florida college student had just found a spot in a parking garage and finished sending texts to her mom. When she got out of her car, she was startled to feel a knife on her throat and to hear: "Do what I say or I'll kill you."

She had a gut feeling that if she went with the man, she would never be coming back. Her immediate response was to fight back with all her might. She grabbed the knife and began kicking and screaming. She used her legs to push off on a parked car and they both ended up on the ground, with the predator losing the knife during the struggle. She managed to kick the predator and to get to her feet and run to safety.

A woman in California was walking through a parking lot in a shopping center, heading to meet some friends for dinner. Suddenly a man drove up dangerously close to her and stuck a handgun out of the window, demanding that she get in his car. She ran from him, screaming, entered the nearest store, and called the police.

Statistically, both women were correct to think that if the predator got them into his car, the likelihood of their survival would have been minimal. The advice I give my students, self-defense instructors, friends, and loved ones is, "In a stranger abduction situation I would rather you do the opposite of what he tells you to do. If he tells you to get in the car, run. If he tells you not to scream, scream as loud as you can. If he tells you don't fight, fight back with all of your might."

In an abduction, a predator does not want to kill you at the initial crime scene and it is not likely that he will. His intent is to get you to a secondary crime scene, where he will brutalize you and probably kill you. When you fight back, scream, or run, you ruin his plan. He has a vision of how his crime will play out, relying on the compliant fear factor. His goal is to instill enough fear in you to cause you to comply with his wishes. Predators seek out soft targets because they imagine it will be easier to scare them into doing what they want and they expect less resistance than from a hard target.

For every woman who finds herself in this situation, it is a personal decision on how to react because your ultimate objective is to survive.

Create a Blueprint

1. Imagine someone pointing a gun at you or putting a knife to your throat and saying something like, "Do what I tell you or I'll kill you."

2. Let yourself feel the fear and rage you would have upon hearing these words.

3. See yourself fighting back with all your might so you don't get taken to a secondary crime scene.

4. Yell, scream, create as much noise as you can to attract attention.

5. See yourself running away, toward people.

6. When you are able to reach your cell, call 911 immediately. Do not call your parents, your significant other, or your best friend first.

Robbery

A young actress, Nancy, and her friends had just finished a night out and were headed home from a bar on New York City's Lower East Side when they were approached by a group of teens looking for trouble and quick cash. They were robbed and Nancy's boyfriend was pistol-whipped for resisting. After the robbery, Nancy challenged the leader of the gang, saying, "What're you still doing here? You got what you wanted. What're you going to do now, shoot us?" The man shot Nancy in the chest, killing her instantly.

Robbery is the forcible stealing of property that increases in severity when aggravating factors are present, such as use of a weapon, and when there is more than one participant. Although robbery can occur anywhere, it is typically a big-city crime. The most common forms of robbery are street robbery and strong-arm robbery, and the most popular weapon is a gun, followed by a knife. Strong-arm tactics include kicking, punching, pushing, and threatening. Most robberies occur at night, between 8 p.m. and 3 a.m.

Robbers working alone or as a pair prefer isolated areas, lone victims, good escape routes, and few witnesses. This is a crime of opportunity. Most robbers don't plan much, give little thought to the possibility of being caught, and rely on the element of surprise.

The predators most likely to commit this crime are urban males between the ages of fifteen and twenty-four. This age group can be very dangerous. Their hormones, specifically testosterone, run high due to their age and they have low levels of self-control. They will often take advantage of the target through sexual assault because they want to exert control and domination over a helpless victim. Very importantly, they are trying to establish their reputation. Looking at a person incorrectly can get you beaten, or stabbed, or worse. When Nancy challenged the robber, his credibility on the street would have been ruined had he backed down.

Everybody knows someone who's been mugged. The best defense is to be alert and attentive to your surroundings and present yourself as a hard target. And if you are mugged, do not fight if it seems the assailant only wants your money. Just hand over your purse or wallet and run.

Create a Blueprint

1. Envision yourself walking home after a night out with friends.
2. You decide to take a shortcut through the park. It's relatively early, and nothing has ever happened there before.
3. A man looms up on you, demanding your purse.
4. You throw it at him and run out of the park, toward people.

Keep the Green and Gold at Home

There are a few factors that make you an obvious target. Flashing wads of cash around is obviously never a good idea. Neither is opening your wallet to rummage for exact change, exposing the big pile of bills you just took out of the ATM. You can also attract unwanted attention by wearing expensive jewelry or watches. It doesn't mean you shouldn't do it, but if you do, you should attempt to keep your jewelry covered or hidden. If you are going out for the evening and wearing sparkly jewelry, hide it under your coat or put it in your purse until you get to your destination. Similarly, you may wear statement necklaces or bracelets to work, and they might not even be real, but a criminal doesn't know that. Keep them out of sight until you get to the office. When you are on public transportation or changing locations (such as getting into or out of your car), especially when wearing jewelry, be extra mindful of your surroundings and on the lookout for anyone who may be watching or scanning for an easy target.

Demonstrations/Protests/Flash Mobs

The original flash mob was usually a large public gathering where people performed an unusual or seemingly random act, such as dancing as a group, and then dispersed. It was typically organized via the Internet or social media. Today flash mobs have turned into roving bands of thugs, rioting, stealing, and assaulting shoppers, patrons, or anyone else who gets in their way. They can be extremely violent.

On December 26, 2016, thousands participated in fifteen flash mob riots across the country, disrupting post-Christmas shopping. The riots occurred in North Carolina, Tennessee, Colorado, Illinois, New York, Ohio, Pennsylvania, and New Jersey. In some cases, SWAT teams were called in.

How do you avoid getting caught in a violent flash mob?

Create a Blueprint

1. Imagine noticing a large group of teens or young adults congregating en masse in a public place, loitering and scanning.

2. Start moving away, preferably toward an exit.

3. Do not attempt to exit your location by walking through the mob. Stay on the edges.

4. If you are caught in the crowd when trouble breaks out, seek shelter in a store. If the mob enters the store, the clerks will flee to the storage areas. Go with them.

5. Don't attempt to fight back; keep your hands up and chin down, keep moving.

6. Keep your back close to the wall to minimize the angles at which you could be attacked.

7. Walk, don't run. Keep your footing solid. If you fall, there is a good chance you will be trampled.

The same tactics can be applied to protests. If you are participating in a peaceful protest that becomes violent, remove yourself from the area. If agitators are present, the likelihood of violence or damage to property is elevated. Keep calm and begin moving in the direction opposite of trouble. If you choose to remain and the police get involved, there is a chance you could be caught up in a mass arrest. The best place for you to be as a protestor is on the outskirts, where it is less likely that you will be caught in the crowd.

Choosing a Contractor

A thirty-five-year-old physician was completing a fellowship at the Children's Hospital of Philadelphia when she hired an exterminator to deal with a rodent issue at her home. During the course of his work she questioned his competence, even stating, "You shouldn't be an exterminator. You don't know what you're doing."

That was all that was needed to set him off. Throwing her on the ground, he straddled and choked her. Police investigators later discovered that he was not even licensed by the state to work as an exterminator.

Use common sense when scheduling work with contractors. Start by checking them out with the Better Business Bureau. The BBB can confirm that they are a legitimate business and will provide a rating; you can also see if there have been any complaints filed against them. Use only established local businesses when possible. For example, you can go to your local hardware store and ask them for recommendations for a plumber. Run a quick Internet search on the company, and ask ahead of time for the name of the worker who will be showing up at your home. If you are hiring contractors for major renovations, you will want to check references, and many companies keep files on their workers. These files contain information such as employment history and a background check. Security cameras or nanny cams are always a good idea. If valuables go missing, a camera can help answer any questions, and a contractor will be identifiable in a recording.

When you allow a contractor into your home, especially if it is only the two of you, you are automatically in a situation that provides a predator with isolation and control. Ideally, you would schedule a contractor visit when someone is with you, though that is not always possible. In that case, let someone know that a contractor is coming to your home.

Create a Blueprint

1. When you greet the contractor at the door, say, "Oh, I was expecting my (mom, friend, husband)." This will put him on notice that you will not be alone for long.

2. Make a phone call within earshot of the contractor and say, "Yes, I have ABC Pest Control at my house."

3. Take a covert picture of him and send it to a friend who knows in advance that you will be doing so. This can be used as a bargaining tool should something happen. Every criminal fears getting caught, and if he knows that he is identifiable, his behavior may be modified.

Elevator Safety

Elevators usually feel safe, especially when you are with coworkers or in your apartment building, but they are attractive to predators because they provide isolation and control. Statistics concerning the risk of elevator crime are hard to come by. Crime and assault rates are higher in residential buildings as compared to commercial buildings because the latter are more likely to have a bell person or security personnel, security cameras, and, generally, more foot traffic. In urban areas, especially in public housing, the rate of criminal activity is very high.

Create a Blueprint

1. Always stand with your back to a wall.

2. Try to stand next to the control panel and alarm.

3. Try not to allow anyone to stand behind you.

4. If the door opens and your intuition tells you that something is not right, don't get in. You can say, "Excuse me," and walk away.

5. If the elevator stops at the basement or roof, never allow yourself to be pulled out. This is the same as being taken to a secondary location in an abduction.

6. Drop to the floor, kick up into the groin region, and use your feet to prevent yourself from being pulled off the elevator. Make as much noise as you can.

Home Invasion/Burglary

One of the more frightening and potentially dangerous crimes that can happen to you and your family is a home invasion. A home invasion is when criminals force their way into an occupied home, apartment, or hotel room to commit a robbery or other crimes. It is particularly frightening because it violates us in a place we consider a safe haven.

According to the Department of Justice, an estimated 3.7 million burglaries occur each year, and in approximately 28 percent of those cases, a household member is present. Once inside, the criminals have what they desire most: isolation and control.

Residential burglaries happen most frequently during the day, when no one is at the house. Home invasions occur more often during evening hours and on weekends.

A home invasion transpires because the criminal believes that you have something of value inside. A person who enters your home knowing that you are there is very dangerous. Women living alone and wealthy seniors are often seen as soft targets. Thieves will also zero in on people in shopping centers, where they observe women who wear high-end clothing or valuable jewelry and drive expensive cars. They will follow them to their homes and attain entry while the woman is moving from the car to the house. Her guard will be down once she reaches her home, and often she will be carrying bags from the shopping trip and be distracted.

How They Enter Your Home

A criminal will break into a home by taking advantage of a weak door or unsecured window. All exterior doors need to be sturdy to decrease the possibility of any of them being kicked or pushed in. You will want solid wood doors, or at the very least doors with a solid wood core. Other options are to install fiberglass or metal doors. Many interior doors, especially to bathrooms or bedrooms, are hollow. Whatever room you use as a safe room should have a dense door.

A door is only as strong as its lock. Even the strongest, most reinforced door can be compromised by one swift kick if the lock does not extend deep enough into the door frame. When choosing a dead bolt, go with a brand name and don't choose the cheapest model.

Frame and Doorjamb

The frame and doorjamb are often overlooked. These two elements are essential to door security—a weak frame and an insubstantial doorjamb will compromise your safety. Instead of a thin, flimsy strike plate, install a deeper box strike (a type of steel pocket that houses the bolt part of your dead bolt). Affix three-inch screws that burrow deep into the wall studs, instead of just the doorjamb. You should also reinforce the doorjamb with galvanized steel to withstand shoulders, kicks, and other attempts to break the door in.

Sliding Glass Doors

Criminals often think of sliding glass doors as invitations, but there is much you can do to secure these decorative entry points. First, make sure your doors are made of reinforced glass or plastic, and not simply thin glass. Always keep them locked. Place a wooden or metal dowel in the track—the rod should measure no more than one-fourth of an inch less than the track length—to prevent the doors from being opened by force.

Windows

Acrylic windows known as Plexiglas are the same thickness as traditional glass while being ten times stronger. Polycarbonate windows are more expensive but are very secure—they're 250 times more impact resistant than safety glass and more than ten times stronger than Plexiglas. Properly installing 12mm film laminate on your windows will reinforce them tremendously against someone attempting to break one to gain entry.

Burglar Alarms

I suggest that burglar alarms be considered an additional—but not the only—level of protection. They can notify you that your home has been compromised, allowing you to react or retreat to a safe place, and they serve as a deterrent. Burglars do not want to attract attention by triggering a siren. However, multiple false alarms will desensitize your neighbors and the police. The wind, an animal, or even a power surge can set off a security system.

Systems range from do-it-yourself kits that you can pick up for ten dollars to sophisticated complete home security networks that must be installed by professionals and could cost thousands of dollars. Motion detectors, glass break sensors, and security cameras are also an option. Always have your alarms installed by security professionals.

The Nanny Cam

The nanny cam is an inexpensive security monitor you install on your own, giving you instant access to view your home, pet, and property via your cell phone, computer, or iPad. It offers great peace of mind and you can check it anytime and anywhere. Think of it as a low-tech, low-price device that can answer questions about things that happened when you were not there and that can be used for later identification.

Many home devices, such as the Canary, are connected to you through Wi-Fi and allow you to see and hear live stream on a 1080p HD camera equipped with auto night vision and high-quality audio. The device is equipped with a siren, motion-activated recording, and other features.

A second option is a Wi-Fi enabled video doorbell like Ring. Ring and devices like it also have infrared cameras and will allow you to speak to anyone at your door from your smartphone, tablet, or PC. It can be programmed to alert you when the doorbell is pressed or by motion activation. You can also add additional cameras.

The Safe Room

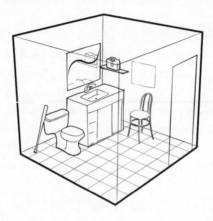

Regardless of whether you live in a house, apartment, condo, or dorm, you need to have a designated safe room, a place that you can go to in a time of crisis. There is not a single thing we have discussed about home safety that is an end-all to keeping you safe, but each suggestion you implement is another layer of protection. A safe room can be as simple as a bathroom with a door reinforcement bar or a safety bar. A safety bar goes under the doorknob and wedges at the bottom of the door, strengthening the flimsiest of doors. However, it will be less effective with hollow doors. It can be purchased at most hardware stores for fewer than twenty-five dollars. At home you can create a safe room using a reinforced walk-in closet. These are high-end and are usually constructed by a security professional or a knowledgeable carpenter. Regardless of whether you spend twenty-five dollars or twenty-five thousand dollars on a safe room, it should contain a safety kit that will include:

- A prepaid cell phone and charger. Purchase an inexpensive phone and pay only a few dollars per month to keep it activated.

- A flashlight with an extra set of batteries.

- A first-aid kit.

- A firearm or weapon such as pepper spray. See the Tigerlight D.A.D. in Chapter 7, under weapons.

If you live at home with family or have roommates, you can have a signal for letting everyone know that there is danger. For instance, the phrase

"Code red!" could indicate that everyone should run to the safe room. You can come up with anything, but keep it short and simple.

Create a Blueprint

1. Imagine you see the shape of a stranger looming at your front door and the handle is rattling. You hear him kicking at the entry.

2. Grab your cell phone.

3. Run to your safe room.

4. Lock the door. Put the safety bar under the doorknob.

5. Dial the local police department. Remember, you should have your police department phone number for where you live and where you work entered into your favorites so that you can call them directly, by pressing one button.

6. Practice repeating your address and a landmark or a cross street out loud.

Active Shooter

Shopping malls, movie theaters, schools, public festivals, airports, places of worship, and vacation spots are where we go to shop, relax, and get away from our everyday routines. Yet they all have something in common. As relatively unprotected locations where people congregate, they are soft targets.

An active shooter is an individual purposefully engaged in killing or attempting to kill people in a confined and populated area. In most cases, a firearm is used though it is not the only weapon that has been used. The weapon of choice for a mass killer extends beyond a firearm to unconventional or improvised weapons. A knife, a hammer, a motor vehicle, explosives, and gasoline have been used to kill.

The motivation might be revenge or to further a political or religious agenda, or they may suffer from a mental illness. Regardless, they all share one thing in common: the intent to kill as many people as possible in the shortest amount of time possible.

The average police response time for emergency calls varies across the country. Response time can be from under five minutes to well above the ten-minute mark, and in some parts of the country it could be much longer. Most active-shooter events are over in minutes.

You are your own first line of defense. What you do in the first seconds of an attack will likely determine whether you are a survivor or a statistic. Whenever you leave your house, you need to be in the yellow zone (heart rate normal but in an alert state) and have a blueprint in the back of your mind.

Believe Your Eyes and Ears

Your eyes and ears are your first defense in detecting danger. Your brain will always try to make instant sense of a situation and will rely on past experience as a guide. So, unless you've been around gunfire, your brain may translate it into something like a car backfiring or fireworks. In Nice, France, on Bastille Day in 2016, a nineteen-ton truck was driven into the crowd of celebrating pedestrians. The truck drove approximately 1.1 miles, killing 86 people and injuring 434. Many weren't able to process the warning sounds of the truck's engine revving, the people screaming, and the masses attempting to move out of the way. They saw and heard what was happening but because it was so unexpected, they did not believe their eyes and ears.

In early January 2017, a man at Florida's Fort Lauderdale International Airport picked up his checked bag from the baggage carousel, took out a

9mm handgun, and began shooting. After the first shots were fired, sur-veillance video captured approximately twelve people in proximity to the shooter when he began his rampage. Nearly all of them temporarily froze, and ten seconds later all of them had hit the floor. They were still within feet from where the shooting had started.

Had the shooter returned to the luggage carousel, he would have had stationary targets, in the form of the people on the ground. Hitting the ground would have been the correct choice only if law enforcement had engaged the gunman and shots were exchanged. In cases like that, you hit the floor and seek cover or do a low crawl to something that will shield you from the gunfire. But when shooting starts in a public place, you can't go wrong by using the Nike defense: run like hell in the opposite direction.

The Hollywood Effect—Take #1

The Virginia Tech shooting, also known as the Virginia Tech massacre, oc-curred on April 16, 2007, in Blacksburg, Virginia. A senior at Virginia Tech shot and killed thirty-two people and wounded seventeen. The students who were shot and killed in the classrooms were all hit three or more times.

Investigators learned that two weeks earlier, the shooter had practiced hitting targets on the ground, knowing that during an attack the students would most likely hit the floor and try to hide. In a movie or television show everyone hits the floor, hides under a desk, or tries to crawl into a corner when the bad guy enters a room. That's exactly what the shooter encountered. The majority of people who were killed obviously thought that that was the correct thing to do. We mimic what we see on television and in the movies. You need to train your brain to accept the horrible reality that in an active-shooter situation there are only limited choices: get shot, fight back, or play dead and hope for the best. Most research points to the best tactic being a group effort to overtake the assailant.

Run

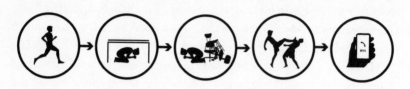

When you hear the sound of gunfire, you need to remove yourself from the location immediately. If you are shot with a handgun, your survival rate is above 80 percent if you get to the hospital within a reasonable amount of time. The main cause of death from a gunshot wound is blood loss, so it is important to control it by applying direct pressure to the wound.

Get Off the X

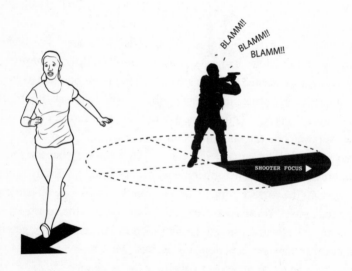

BLAMM!!
BLAMM!!
BLAMM!!

SHOOTER FOCUS ▶

The immediate area where the shooting is taking place is referred to as the kill zone. The X is the area directly in front of and slightly to the shooter's left and right. The farther you take yourself off the kill zone, the more you increase your chance of surviving. However, if you can hear gunshots, you can be shot. Run away in a zigzag or irregular pattern. It is easier for a shooter to target you in a straight line than in an irregular pattern of movement, and it is much harder to hit a moving target than a stationary one. Stay away from the wall. A bullet can ricochet off it and continue to travel.

Create a Blueprint

1. The first thing to do when you go to a public place, such as a shopping mall, is to locate the nearest exits.

2. Visualize the sound of gunfire and see yourself running immediately in the opposite direction. You may know that another store has an exit into the parking structure. In a classroom building, you may know that there's a stairwell that leads to the lower floors.

Hide/Barricade

The upscale Westgate Mall in Nairobi, Kenya, was the scene of a terrorist attack in September 2013 when gunmen stormed the shopping complex, killing people as they encountered them. In all, sixty-seven people were killed. Many of those who survived did so by playing dead, barricading themselves in storerooms, or hiding in boxes and utility closets. Typically, in an active-shooter situation, the shooter is looking to kill and knows that he doesn't have much time. He will not stop and search every closet or look under every desk. Nor will he waste time attempting to force his way into a locked room or office. Many rifles don't even have the capability to shoot through solid doors or locks.

If you find yourself in an area in which the exits are blocked, your next-best option is to hide or barricade yourself. This may be particularly necessary if you are trapped in a school or office building.

Barricade yourself in a room by locking the door and placing heavy items in front of it if available. Be sure to turn out the lights, remain quiet, and turn your cell phone to silent. You can also use your body to brace against the items you have placed in front of the barricade. Sit low and be sure there are ample solid objects between you and the door.

Create a Blueprint

1. The first thing you do when you go to a public place, such as an office building, is to locate the nearest exits.

2. Visualize the sound of gunfire and realize the gunshots are between you and the exit.

3. In a mall, you may seek shelter in a storage room.

4. Many classroom doors on both high school and college campuses now have locks. See yourself running into a room and locking the door. Turn off the lights and stay out of view of the door window.

5. In a classroom or office building, run into a room and use chairs, desks, and file cabinets to barricade the door. Be sure you see yourself using a table or file cabinet to cover a glass window, if there is one.

Fight Back

Once a shooter begins the carnage, there is no reasoning with him. Absolutely none. If you have no other option but to fight back, you must do so without hesitation and with full intensity. Doing nothing will be fatal.

Create a Blueprint

1. Envision hearing the gunman coming your way.

2. Search for anything that can be used as a weapon: a fire extinguisher, a pair of scissors, a sharpened pencil, or a steel point or needlepoint pen.

3. See yourself attack the shooter with full force and fury.

4. Envision nothing else but perseverance and victory.

TAKEAWAYS

- Like any encounter with someone who intends you harm, the first ten to twenty seconds are critical in determining your survivability/escapability.

- Visualize in vivid detail each scenario.

- Revisit and update the self-defense files when you think of a new scenario or challenge. This might be sparked by something that happens to someone you know or from hearing about a crime in the media. Ask yourself, "How would I have handled that?" Create a blueprint and file it away, just in case.

7
SELF-DEFENSE

■ ■ ■ ■ ■ ■ ■ ■ ■ ■

- One out of every six women has been the target of rape or an attempted rape in her lifetime.
- A rape happens once every 98 minutes in the United States.
- You will know the rapist 70 percent of the time.
- The majority of sexual assaults occur at or near the home.

While official statistics give the number of women who have been subject to attempted or completed rape as one out of six, when you speak with people who work on the front lines of sexual assault, such as nurses, doctors, and other medical professionals, mental health workers, members of the law enforcement community, counselors, psychologists, and women's health activists, there is widespread agreement that the numbers are much higher. Sexual assault is one of the most underreported crimes in the United States. A 2007 Department of Justice study of college students showed that fewer than 5 percent of victims report rape or attempted rape to the police. A more accurate figure could be that one out of every four women has been the target of an attempted or completed rape.

I hope you will never have to use the techniques or utilize the weapons reviewed in this chapter. Use of force and violence is always the last resort. You turn to it when you have tried everything else and have no other alternatives. The first step to protecting yourself begins with your intuition. It is reinforced when you present yourself as a hard target and understand and adopt the concept of situational awareness. It is knowing that any time you are out and about, you should be in the yellow zone—your heart rate is normal, yet you are alert to and observant of the world around you. You have the ability to detect pre-indicators, meaning you notice when someone seems to be evaluating you and you register facial expressions that don't fit in. You have become adept at spotting abnormal behavior. All these steps will keep you and your family safe most of the time.

Bad people will seek out soft targets. They use surprise to their advantage and will pick a person who they don't think will resist or fight back. Just as I did in social experiments on college campuses and in nightclubs,* a predator will assess your body language within a few seconds and decide if you are easy to intimidate and control. If you have been mistaken for a soft target, you have to fight back with determination and effective techniques so that they know immediately that they have picked the wrong woman.

The Nike Defense

Whenever you can, use the Nike defense: run like hell. If that doesn't work, always fight back.

Always Fight Back

Studies have indicated that half of all attackers will break off their attack if a woman resists and fights back. *Half of all attackers.* By making it difficult from the get-go, you are making yourself a more difficult target. Department of Justice studies also show that women who resist are not injured any more than are women who don't resist. I can't repeat it enough: if running isn't an option, always fight back.

A Sexual Predator Needs Two Conditions to Achieve His Goals

For sexual assault, a predator needs to achieve isolation and control. In the case of an acquaintance, he may already have that. He may be visiting you at home or in your dorm. In the case of a stranger, he wants to get you somewhere isolated, where no one else can help or intervene. This is known

* In an experiment I did with the undercover investigative unit at *Inside Edition*, I approached five women in a New York City nightclub with a mixed drink. They all accepted the drink from me, a total stranger, and consumed it. Had it contained a date rape drug, they would have been compromised.

as the secondary location. His method to achieve that can be through home invasion, carjacking, or kidnapping. Once you are alone with him, he has a distinct advantage. If he restrains you, he will have complete control.

A Predator Has Two Fears

Predators fear being caught and they fear getting hurt. The purpose of fighting back is not to beat the predator to a pulp and win but rather to change his behavior by hurting him enough so you can escape. Also, it is to let him know that you intend to cause a lot of noise and get attention so that he runs the risk of getting caught. When you are selected by a predator, it is because he believes that you are a soft target and that he can overpower you with minimum risk to himself. On countless occasions, surveillance footage has shown that when a woman screams and fights, a predator will not spend much time attempting to overpower her. He will often abandon his efforts and look for an easier target if he is not successful in the first twenty or thirty seconds.

When you make noise, it attracts attention and increases the chances someone will come to your aid or call the police. Please be aware that you cannot assume that anyone will actually come to help—that is not a realistic action plan—but a predator likely will not stick around to see if someone shows up and increase his risk of getting caught.

The Compliant Fear Factor

The predator will rely on your fear to get you to do what he wants. I refer to this as the compliant fear factor. He will say anything he deems necessary to move you to a secluded area. He wants you to think that all you need to do is listen to him and he will eventually let you go. You will want to believe it, too, because the alternative is unthinkable.

It is the furthest thing from the truth, however. Statistically, it is not likely that he will release you if he gets you under his control in an isolated location. The probability of you coming back is very slim.

This scenario can play out in an acquaintance or stranger abduction, but it is more likely to occur in a stranger situation. Whoever it is, he wants you to stop resisting and not fight back. Thus he will try to instill fear in you through threats, to get you to do what he wants. He may display a weapon and order you to get into his car.

He will say things to you like:

- "Do what I say or I will kill you."
- "Do what I say and you will not be hurt."
- "Don't scream or I will kill you."

These words should serve as a trigger to you that it is not very likely that he can accomplish his objectives at point A (where you currently are) and he needs to get you to point B (somewhere else), where he has isolation and control. He definitely does not want to get caught, nor does he want to get injured. Doing the opposite of what he tells you to do, such as screaming, struggling, and fighting back, plays upon those fears and will ruin his plans.

The Six Basic Self-Defense Principles

1. Pay Attention to the People Around You

When you are on the go, be sure to scan and monitor your surroundings. Be alert and observant, listen to your intuition, and if something catches your attention as unusual, watch it until you are certain it is not a threat. Predators will exhibit pre-indicators, behaviors that show they are preparing to act out. They may engage you in conversation, sometimes known as "interviewing." Their facial expressions will also provide clues to their intentions.

2. Stay with People or Go to People

Do not let yourself be taken somewhere else. If you do, you will live your worst nightmare, because there will be no one to help you. If you are in a parking lot or a mall, at a party, or anywhere there are people around, do not go with the predator. Conversely, if you are alone in your house or in an office, go to people. Run outside, climb out your window, drive to a convenience store—but go where there are people.

3. Keep a Barrier Between You and the Bad Guy

Lock your doors. Don't open the door for anyone you don't know. Stay in your car; push a shopping cart in the parking lot. Keep something in between you and him. Anything that requires more time and effort for him to get to you increases his chances of being discovered. It also gives you extra time to fight back or escape. If the predator doesn't have isolation and control, then he sees time as the adversary. The clock is ticking and he doesn't want to get caught.

4. Attract Attention

More than 90 percent of all predators will say something like "Don't scream or I'll kill you" or "Stay quiet and you won't get hurt." They are telling you exactly what will ruin their plan. Honk the horn, scream, kick, throw an object, and break windows in order to attract attention.

5. Control His Hips and Control His Hands

You are controlling the distance between the two of you and preventing penetration when you control his hips. His hands can hurt you by choking, hitting, or stabbing. When you hold them using the methods depicted in this chapter, you limit his ability to injure you.

6. Take Advantage of a Woman's Strengths When You Fight

Don't try to fight a man like a man. If you punch a predator in the face, he's going to punch you back with even more power, possibly breaking your nose or even knocking you out. Use your strongest weapons against his weakest targets. You will kick and use elbows and knees against his face, throat, and groin. Head-butts, strikes to the eyes, and biting are addressed in more intermediate and advanced lessons.

The Truth About Violence

Real-world violence is fast and ugly. It is not gracefully choreographed and there is absolutely nothing pretty about it. You will not expect it when it does happen.

When I teach recruits in the police academy, the young officers, both men and women who have never been punched in the face before, usually have the same reaction. Their expressions are shock: they are stunned by the white-light flashes that accompany a blow to the head, and they drop their hands away from their faces instead of moving them up for cover.

YOUR TARGET IS HIS CENTER LINE
ELBOW AND KNEE STRIKES

For women, elbow and knee strikes are power moves that are most effective in close quarters. You will come up short if you attempt to trade punches with a man. I broke my hand wearing eight-ounce gloves while boxing, but as a police officer I have used elbow and knee strikes in the field with great effectiveness.

Notorious rapist and murderer John Gardner, who sexually assaulted and killed two teenage girls in Southern California, is serving two consecutive life sentences plus an additional twenty-five-years-to-life for the attempted rape of a college student. The student was home on break when Gardner tackled her and threatened to rape her on a running trail. She fought back, hitting him in the nose with a right elbow strike. It was that strike that saved her life. She credits fighting back, having self-defense training, and the grace of God for the fact that she was able to escape from him.

Even their police academy training does not prepare them for the reality of a real-life encounter. If you are attacked, your first instinct may be to comply immediately with whatever the predator wants because you will not want to be hit again.

The Hollywood Effect—Take #2

Most people in their lifetime will see thousands of acts of violence—all of them on television or in the movies, with little resemblance to

Horizontal Elbow Strike

- In this technique, a woman will rotate her body, swing her elbow forward, and strike the attacker with it.

- This technique is often combined with grasping an opponent's head so the opponent cannot move away from the elbow strike.

- The bend in the wrist will allow for a more effective strike.

- The front knee strike is a good follow-up technique.

Front Knee Strike

- In this technique, a woman will thrust her knee into the groin or lower abdomen of the attacker.

- This technique is often combined with grasping an opponent's shoulder(s) so the opponent cannot move away from the knee strike and for better accuracy.

- It is important to drive the hips forward and point the toes to the ground.

- The horizontal elbow strike is a good follow-up technique.

genuine violence. The fights and gun battles we do see are creative and sequenced to entertain us. You see things such as the good guy effortlessly shooting a gun out of the bad guy's hand, or a lone hero with a handgun killing three thugs carrying automatic weapons, or a police officer taking an evil criminal into custody in under five seconds, with stealth and precision.

In reality, violence is messy and scary and complicated. It is behavior involving physical force that is intended to significantly hurt or kill someone. While a single shot is portrayed as enough to kill someone instantaneously in the movies and on TV, the truth is that you can be shot in the heart or in the head and still function for ten seconds or even live. Shots are fatal in only 20 percent of your body. If you get shot elsewhere you could slowly bleed out, but death is rarely instantaneous.

The Dynamics of a Sexual Assault

In a sexual assault, you will be grabbed or dragged somewhere (such as an adjacent room or a car, or a secondary location) that is isolated. If sexual assault is the intent at that very moment, you will likely be brought to the ground within five seconds or less. In the first ten seconds, a criminal will use all his strength, force, and rage to get you under his control. In fact, the first ten seconds are considered so critical that years ago, officers were encouraged to unleash ten seconds of uncontrolled violence to overwhelm a resisting criminal. This type of language is no longer used but the concept of a quick reaction remains.

Similarly, the first twenty seconds of an attack are absolutely critical. An escape can still be made during that brief period (though it will feel endless). The longer you are in close confines with the predator, the higher the risk of getting hurt or compromised.

If you are unfamiliar with close combat, you will be at a huge disadvantage. Similarly, if you have no self-defense knowledge to fall back on, you are vulnerable. Solid, realistic self-defense techniques will make all the difference.

The Predators

The term *date rape* is sometimes used to refer to acquaintance rape, and approximately seven out of ten sexual assaults are committed by an intimate partner or an acquaintance. A perpetrator of acquaintance rape might be a date, but he could also be a classmate, a neighbor, a friend's significant other, or in any number of roles. It's important to remember that dating, instances of past intimacy, or other acts such as kissing do not give someone consent for increased or continued sexual contact.

In other instances, a woman may not know the perpetrator at all. This type of sexual violence is sometimes referred to as stranger rape and can occur in several different ways. The main ones:

BLITZ SEXUAL ASSAULT: This occurs when a perpetrator quickly and brutally assaults a woman, with no prior contact, usually at night in a public place. The blitz is a surprise attack.

CONTACT SEXUAL ASSAULT: A perpetrator contacts a woman and tries to gain her trust by flirting, luring her to his car, or otherwise trying to coerce her into a situation where the sexual assault will occur.

HOME INVASION SEXUAL ASSAULT: When a stranger breaks into the woman's home to commit the assault.

How Safe Are You?

To prevent a worst-case scenario, you should be able to say "Yes" to the situations below. Try to practice them, if appropriate. At the very least, visualize yourself going through the motions and making your escape.

- Can you get out of a room if someone is blocking the door?
  Have someone large get between you and the door. Experience how it feels to try to get around him or make him move.

- Can you struggle hard enough not to let someone pick you up or drag you away?
  Ask someone strong to pick you up and see how you respond as you try to get out of his grasp.

- Can you get hit in the head and recover fast enough to figure out how to get away?
  If you are in good physical condition and it is something you want to experience, consider putting on a pair of boxing gloves with a trained self-defense instructor. Experience what it is like to trade punches with someone. Note: You don't have to get hit in the head.

- Can you open the door of a car quickly and roll out even if it is moving?
  Don't practice this move. Do visualize it.

- Can you get into your car quickly, without panicking, if you feel like someone is closing in on you?
  Practice getting in and out of your car as fast as you can.

Defend University

Defend University is a research and development group that is dedicated to establishing and creating cutting-edge tactics, techniques, and strategies for women's safety, law enforcement, and campus safety.

Women sign up for our self-defense programs to become better at fighting back. Regardless of whether it is a three-hour seminar, preparing high school seniors for freshman year at college, or women who go through our eight- or twelve-week program, we have never failed to meet that goal.

Our motto is "Fight Like a Woman," which means that a woman brings her strengths to the conflict (trunk muscles/lower body) while minimizing the strengths of a man by not affording him the opportunity to punch her in the face or the head. Your brain is the control center, and should it be traumatized or damaged, your ability to function will also be impaired. Using your legs to kick from the safety position (demonstrated later in this chapter), with the ground as your base, you can hurt a man two or three times your size.

We have had our instructors who play "the bad guys" by wearing thick, padded suits be knocked unconscious by girls weighing less than 100 pounds. From the safety position, a man's most vulnerable part, his centerline, can be accessed. It is the area from his groin to his nose and is available to your kicks. I've included more about Defend University at the end of the book.

This Is Not a Martial Arts Program

I was investigating a sexual assault case in which an acquaintance forcibly raped a woman in her early thirties. After a SANE nurse (Sexual Assault Nurse Examiner) collected the forensic evidence and began the recovery process, it was my job to interview the woman. During the course of the investigation, she revealed that she had studied martial arts for more than ten years. She was devastated that her non–martial arts acquaintance, who she believed was a friend, had raped her. When the struggle began, the first thing that went through her mind was "This isn't the way it happens in class." She said to me, "Nothing I had learned worked and I felt defenseless."

She described extreme fear when she was attacked, far beyond what she expected to feel in such a situation. She was also further devastated by the confusion of not being able to stop the attack. Her training had not sufficiently prepared her and she was stunned by her inability to thwart the attacker.

What is in this book, and what I teach at Defend University, is not a martial arts program, but rather a woman-specific safety and self-defense program. The majority of our students are not looking for a martial arts program and they would likely never set foot in a dojo or martial arts academy. However, they want self-defense that is simple, easy to learn, easy to remember, and specific to women. The techniques taught in Defend University's women's self-defense program are all gross motor skill movements that are highly effective when you are in the green zone (under attack, heart rate 145 to 175 beats per minute).

Self-Defense Techniques

While I have taught members of the FBI, DEA, U.S. Marshals Service, Navy SEALs, Marines, and Army Rangers, to name a few, this is not an elite military or law enforcement program converted for civilian use. I teach the military and law enforcement differently than the general public and I teach women completely differently than any other group.

The techniques presented here play upon a woman's strengths and are easy to remember in times of stress. They are designed to address common scenarios involving sexual assault and crimes against women. Videos of all the techniques are available on our website at www.DefendUniversity.com. But just because they seem basic and easy to do doesn't mean fighting off an attacker will be effortless and straightforward. It will probably be the hardest thing you have ever done.

Your Self-Defense Objective

Your objective is to cause enough damage to the predator so that you change his behavior to allow you to escape. You may break his nose or cause him serious injury, but your main goal is to get away as fast as you can. You may only need to disable him for a few seconds to do so. That means doing anything that is necessary, including biting, kicking, and head-butting. I will explain how to practice this in the section on "Training the Mind" later in this chapter. You want to train a technique so that it becomes a reaction instead of an action. Experts in the field tell us you need more than 100 repetitions to make a proper engram in the brain. I have seen this number reduced by training the mind and using visualization. Learning off the apperceptive base,* you can easily do 25 to 30 reps in a one-hour class.

How to Practice the Techniques

While working with a group of FBI agents and teaching them defense tactics, I coined the phrase "super-slow motion" and that is how you should start practicing the techniques. In the beginning, go slowly and feel your way through every aspect of the moves. Over time, you will automatically add speed. Through repetition, you will understand how it is supposed to feel when you do it correctly. The subconscious mind will work with you to help you accomplish this.

Rape Escape Position

The kicking technique described opposite is very powerful and can cause a lot of damage. When a man has one or both knees on the ground, he does not have the ability to move or absorb a strike, especially a kick. The kicking part of this position is called the up-kick, and the results are so devastating that it was outlawed in the Ultimate Fighting Championships (UFC) in 2009. To see the effects of an up-kick, do a search on "UFC, up-kick knockouts." You will see dozens of examples of the effectiveness. In this technique, the ground is your base and you are using your trunk muscles to kick upward into his groin, stomach, and face. Kicking from the ground is many times more effective than kicking while standing.

You are in the worst position possible—he has you pinned down to the ground and is between your thighs. Rape is imminent (see position #1 opposite).

Brace your hands on his shoulders and slide your hips out. You won't be able to move him, so move yourself. If he has your wrists pinned, you can still use your feet to push your hips out. Once you have slid your hips out, place your feet on his hips. Don't put them on his thighs; he'll just fall

---

* The apperceptive base is the mental process by which a person makes sense of an idea by assimilating it into the body of ideas she already possesses. Simply put, it means taking a previously learned skill and applying it to a newly learned skill.

Rape escape position #1

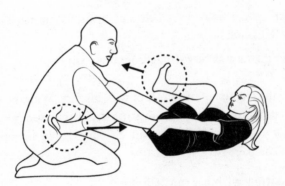

Rape escape position #2

on you. With one foot still on his hip, bring the other leg back (your knee to your chest) and kick his closest body part, which will most likely be his face. (See illustration above for body alignment.) Now ride the bicycle, kicking him along the centerline. If his head is thrown back, the next-closest target will likely be his stomach or groin. He's on his knees and stuck in slow-motion mode; use this to your advantage (see position #2 above).

Bonus: As you move your hips away, slide your hands from his chest down his arms to his wrists. Keep your palms down and broaden your knees so that they touch your thumbs; that will help support your grip. All you need is one second. With one foot pressed into his hip and holding his wrists, you can't miss, not even if your eyes were closed. No matter what happens, keep kicking.

Once you have knocked him out or back, get up and escape. Place both of your hands on the floor to either your left or right side and hop up to your feet in a tripod or a position much like a child would take when first learning to stand up. This is called standing up in base and is the most efficient way to ensure you have the stability to flee.

Note: Most women, in a time of stress, will try to stand up and begin running before they have their footing, causing them to fall or trip over their own legs.

Advantages of the Defensive Position

- Your weapons (your kicks) are between you and the bad guy.
- Your head is away from his hits.
- All of his targets are open to your kicks.
- Your legs are always longer than his arms. So you can kick him, but he cannot hit you.
- Your platform is very strong from this position.

Notice the alignment of your foot with his face. With the ground as your base, using your strongest body parts (trunk muscles) to kick up and from below his face is like hitting with a George Foreman uppercut (see position #2 on page 161).

Rape Position with a Front Choke

The choke is a rage move. Anyone who places his hands around your neck means to control you, hurt you, or kill you; there is no simpler way to explain this act of violence. Years ago, if the police responded to a domestic violence call and the woman had marks on or around her neck, the laws were written in such a way that it would only constitute a harassment violation. Today every state that I am aware of has a statute on choking, or "obstruction of breathing or blood circulation." Such an act of aggression is now taken very seriously by law enforcement and prosecutors.

It is common for a rapist to try to choke you into submission, or unconsciousness, using a front choke. This is especially true when he feels you resisting him. Rape is all about power, control, dominance, and humiliation. If you are not complying with him, he may try to choke or hit you.

Rape with front choke position #1

Rape with front choke position #2

- Your first priority is to keep your airway clear. Tuck your chin and raise your shoulders to protect the soft tissue around your neck. This will buy you some time.

- Bring both arms up over the top of his arms.

- Clasp your hands on his wrists and use your arms to secure his arms to your chest. Use your strong back muscles to pull down to give you a little bit of space for your windpipe. Keep your head on the ground (see position #1 above).

- Slide back to allow yourself to place your feet into his hips, then keep one foot on his hip and ride the bicycle into his face (see postion #2 above).

- As you slide back, move your hands on his elbows and then slide your hands to his wrists. Bow knees out and kick.
- Stand up in base and escape.

The Defensive Position

The defensive position relies on the element of surprise and what is known as distance deception. Distance deception gives the predator the belief that you can't reach him but he can reach you. He wants to get close enough to be able to strike you, especially your head. Since people don't usually fight from this range, you will have the advantage. You can reach his groin, stomach, or face. Even professional fighters are not familiar with this range. A good example of this can be seen in the video footage of an MMA event with Renzo Gracie against Oleg Taktarov, a very powerful Russian fighter. Gracie knocked Taktarov flat on his back with a light kick to the face and easily finished his stunned opponent.

- While on your back your legs will be loaded (knees up and slightly bent outward).
- Your back is rounded and you use your elbows and feet to track your aggressor.
- When he gets close, aim your kick to the closest vulnerable target along his centerline.

The defensive position

Controlling Your Space

You own your personal space. It is the comfort zone you create when you are speaking with other people and it will vary from person to person. Your personal space when dealing with a loved one might be very small. When talking to someone in a social setting, you will likely stand at arm's length. If you are in a situation where you feel threatened, you are going to have many feet between you and the other person. As a woman, you might have your space violated every day inadvertently or by people testing your limits. Take control of your boundaries through the Soft Challenge techniques below.

Soft Challenge

When someone violates your space, put him on notice by stepping back or to the side. This is often enough to discourage closeness. If, at the onset of your interaction, you have a gut feeling that you need to be more assertive, bring your hands up to chest level with your fingers together. At this point you don't need to say anything, but you can give him a look as if to say, "SERIOUSLY" (see position #1 below).

Soft challenge position #1

Hard challenge position #1

Hard challenge position #2

Hard Challenge

After you have sent a message using the Soft Challenge technique, a predator with bad intentions may press forward again, upping the ante through
physical confrontation. Step back with your hands up. You've marked

your boundary, you've identified to onlookers who the bad guy is, you've protected your head and it is like an antenna.

Challenge him with "STOP!" or "LEAVE ME ALONE!" or "BACK OFF!" This will attract additional attention and put people on notice that there is a problem.

If he continues to advance close enough to touch your front hand, deliver a palm heel strike to his chin (see position #1 opposite). His head will go backward. If necessary, deliver a strike to the groin with your knee (see position #2 opposite). I like women to grab his shoulders so as to have a reference point for better accuracy. You can follow up with a horizontal elbow strike.

Escape.

Trying to Force You to a Secondary Location

Being taken to a secondary location is an unforgiving scenario. If this is his intent, he will grab your wrist or arm and attempt to pull you (see position #1 below). You will need to base out so you don't go head over heels (see position #2 on page 168).

Avoiding a secondary location position #1

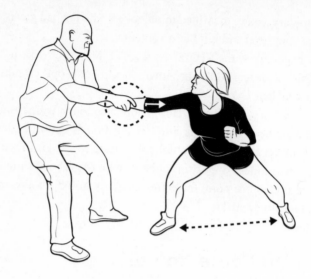

Avoiding a secondary location position #2

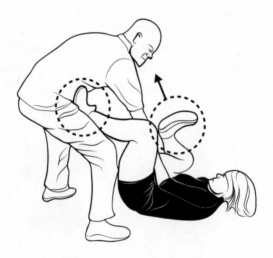

Avoiding a secondary location position #3

■ Do not attempt to strike him when he is pulling you. Your accuracy is critically reduced. You will be off balance and you will feed into the pull.

- Step in and sit down to the defensive position. Hold his arm using both hands (baseball bat grip) and put one of your feet into his hip (see position #3 opposite).

- Push-pull: Push with your foot into his hip and pull his arm toward you. He will be temporarily immobilized, allowing you to kick to the groin or face.

- Escape.

Rear Choke Escape, aka the Blitz

Blitz position #1

Blitz position #2

This is an especially scary attack for two reasons. First, it is a very effective method of overpowering a woman and difficult to escape from. Second, the rapist who feels the need to "blitz" his victim is in many ways more dangerous than the other rapists. Most likely he will be a stranger.

- Your first priority is to maintain a clear airway. Tuck your chin (see position #1 above).

- Reach up and grab his arm with both of your arms. Get one of your hands near his hand and your other hand near his elbow.

- Keep your elbows pinned to your body, use your whole body to weigh down his arm, and make yourself very heavy.

- Turn your head toward the crook of his arm to give you space for your windpipe.

- Step your feet out about six inches. Lower your bottom to where your feet were (see position #2 on page 169).

- Push up on his elbow and spin toward your chin. (Do not put your back flat on the ground. Keep it rounded.)

- Spin into the defensive position and retain his arm using both hands and one of your feet, which goes into his hip. Push with your foot into his hip and pull his arm toward you. He will be temporarily immobilized, allowing you to kick to the groin or face (see position #3 below).

- Escape.

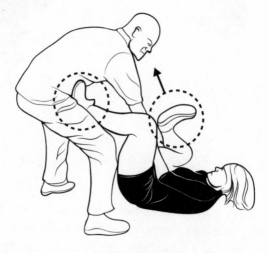

Blitz position #3

Frontal Blitz: Bear Hug Over Arms

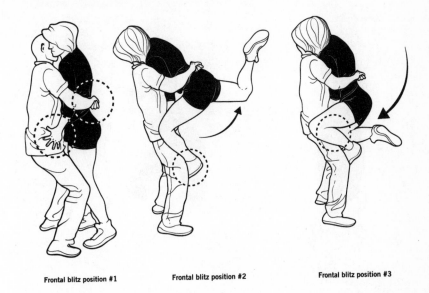

Frontal blitz position #1   Frontal blitz position #2   Frontal blitz position #3

The predator picks you up in a bear hug over your arms to move you from point A to point B. If he gets you to point B, he will be unforgiving.

- Brace your hands on his hips (palm heels) (see position #1 above).

- Point the knee of one leg out and slide your instep up into his upper thigh and brace (see position #2 above).

- Using the leverage from the leg that is anchored (push your hips away), raise the free leg. Deliver a stiff leg kick to the groin. Be prepared to land on your feet, since this is a very effective strike and the predator will likely drop you (see position #3 above).

- Follow up with a horizontal elbow strike if necessary.

- Escape.

The Frame: Unwanted Contact

Frame position #1

Frame position #2

Frame position #3

This is good for a social situation where you are confronted with unwanted attention, for example, if you are at a gathering and you see creepy Uncle

Rob coming toward you. Obviously, he has had a few too many and wants a hug. As he closes in on you:

- Step back and make a frame with your arms. Always use the same side, left foot forward, left arm up and out front (see position #1 opposite).

- The supporting arm should be only slightly bent. The frame should be able to support a considerable amount of pressure and should not collapse when pressure is applied.

- The supporting arm will grab the wrist of your front arm.

- The front arm palm is facing the floor and the blade of your forearm goes into his neck (see position #2 opposite).

- Don't lean. Stay fifty-fifty and let him do all the work. The more he pulls, the more pressure he puts on his own throat.

- If he is persistent, follow up with a knee to the groin and/or elbow to the face (see postion #3 opposite). (If you do this with a partner, make sure your partner bites down on his teeth and tucks his chin or else he may be injured.)

Frame Strike

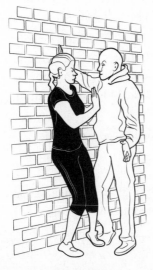

Frame strike position #1

Frame strike position #2

Frame strike position #3

- He's crowding you. Maybe he has you pinned up against the wall but your hands are free and by your upper chest (see position #1 on page 173).

- Just as you did in the last move, grab your wrist with your supporting hand. Your elbows will be tight to your side.

- Thrust the frame upward and under his jaw. There is a lot of force behind the thrust and you could cause significant injury. Aim the frame at his upper chest and continue moving up, using the throat as a guide so that you can't miss (see position #2 on page 173).

- Be prepared to follow up with a knee strike (see position #3 above).

Note: You will have "what-if" questions regarding the techniques. Many are addressed in the demo videos at www.DefendUniversity.com.

Training the Mind

You were born to win, but to be a winner you must plan to win, prepare to win, and expect to win.
—Zig Ziglar

Before using any of the self-defense techniques I have provided, you must believe that you will prevail in an attack. Utilizing the same process that was used to create blueprints for avoiding trouble, de-escalating, or removing yourself from potentially dangerous situations, you can also visualize physical encounters or assaults. The most powerful weapon in the body is the brain and it needs training, too. Train the mind, because it will quit before the body does. You need to have faith that you can overcome any physical confrontation through mental preparation and by learning basic self-defense moves.

You can do all the physical training in the world, yet without visualization, your accomplishments may well be hampered. Although I have never had to resort to deadly force, for most of my career I have visualized thousands of scenarios and identified the fine line between having to use force or not. Without reviewing those thousands of scenarios, I know that I might hesitate to use the force necessary to stop or prevent a threat, and such a hesitation could get myself or another person seriously injured or worse.

Envision someone whom you find scary or intimidating. It could be a gang member or a guy you pass on the street every day who gives you the creeps. That's the guy you want to see yourself fighting. That's the guy you want to dominate. It will slowly build your confidence.

Several factors can hinder your ability to believe you can win during a time of extreme stress.

- You must know some basic self-defense techniques that you can rely upon in a time of need. This chapter introduced several effective techniques.

- You cannot look into the future and predetermine an outcome by thinking to yourself, "That guy is so big," or, "He looks so crazy there is no way I will be able to get away."

- You must have the ability to control the adrenal process so that you do not freeze from fear. When your heart beats at 175 to 200 beats per minute, you can fall into the frozen zone, where you become paralyzed.

Weapons and Improvised Weapons

Hence to fight and conquer in all your battles is not supreme excellence; supreme excellence consists in breaking the enemy's resistance without fighting.

—*Sun Tzu*

A weapon is an object designed to inflict bodily harm or physical damage, like a knife, pepper spray, or a gun. It is used as a means of gaining an advantage or defending yourself in a conflict. An improvised weapon is something that is either on your person, like a pen, or fashioned from something around you, like an umbrella or tightly wrapped newspaper.

While a roll of coins makes for a great improvised weapon, holding your keys between your fingers and hitting another person will likely lead to you injuring or breaking you fingers. Test it out by striking a pillow or a punching bag lightly. You can hold the keys in the palm of your hand and use a hammer or ice-pick striking motion. You will likely cause only surface injuries to the predator.

If you intend to carry any type of a personal defense weapon or device, you need to get training from a qualified professional, especially if you elect to carry a handgun or obtain a long gun for home safety. I respect the debate from both sides regarding the Second Amendment. No matter what you choose as a self-defense option, you must consider the legal, civil, and moral issues surrounding the use of any weapon against another person. Also, keep in mind that anything you hold in your hand can be dropped and any weapon can potentially be used against you. However, practice and proper training will decrease this possibility. I've highlighted a handful of the most common weapons and recommend you at least become familiar with them.

Blunt Force Tools

A blunt force tool can be incorporated into your everyday carry. Many double as key chains and can serve other purposes aside from self-defense. They will be inconspicuous and some (such as tactical pens) are disguised as everyday objects to further avoid detection. If you practice with it regularly and have developed muscle memory to render it effective in an emergency, an item like this will give you an edge in a bad situation. They are commonly referred to as Kubotan.

Pros:

- Better than punching with your hand
- Can be effective in causing injury

Cons:

- Cross-contamination with blood-borne pathogens*

Flashlights

I am an advocate of flashlights for several reasons. Many crimes are committed under the cloak of darkness. Well-known Navy SEAL Ken Good is a low-light expert and creator of the Night Reaper Estrela Flashlight. It has an adjustable recall dim position and puts out 1,000 lumens of strobe light.

At close range, when subjects are dark-adapted, the effect is overwhelming. More often than not, eyes close immediately, heads turn, hands come up, and balance is disrupted.

When subjected to a strobing light, your eye/brain image generation

---

* Blood-borne pathogens are contaminations of bodily fluids that contain microorganisms that are unintentionally transferred from one person to another and include but are not limited to HIV and Hepatitis C.

capability is seriously degraded. You will have an extremely difficult time formulating an accurate picture of reality. "Entertainment folks and those who create haunted houses have been using this phenomenon for years to alter your perception of what is actually happening," Good writes.*

By activating the strobe light effect, you can gain valuable time to escape, or the flashlight can be used as a blunt force weapon.

As an added bonus, what does every cop in America carry at night? A flashlight, and the predator knows this.

Pros:

- Multiuse device
- Powerful strobe feature
- Can be used as a blunt instrument
- Improves vision at night

Cons:

- Should be 500–1,000 lumens to be effective

Needlepoint/Steel Point Pens

It takes very little pressure to penetrate the skin. When I travel, particularly when I fly, I always take several Pilot V5 needlepoint pens and several sharpened No. 2 pencils. Hold the pen or pencil in your hand with a closed fist and your thumb over the top of the pen. The target area on the predator would be the soft tissue of the neck; stab and leave the pen or pencil in his neck. A steel point pen is also a good option.

Pros:

- Can be on your person at all times
- Not seen as a weapon
- Legal

---

* Ken J. Good, "Deployment of Illumination Tools," *Law Enforcement Training Primer,* Copyright © 2014, www.nightreaper.com.

Cons:

- Usually relied upon as a last resort in areas where other, more effective weapons are not allowed, such as on airplanes, in federal buildings, and at other locations that screen for weapons

Pepper Spray

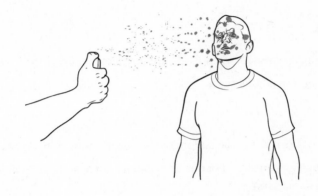

I have been a pepper spray instructor for fifteen years and I am a big advocate of it, especially since it is legal in all fifty states. Do not announce that you have it. You always want it to be a surprise. When you are choosing a pepper spray, consider the following:

- Concentration amounts vary, but law enforcement grade is preferred.
- It should be carried in your hand or on a belt carrier and not in a backpack or pocketbook when you are out and about.
- The most effective pepper spray device will have a handle that allows it to be wrapped around your hand so that you can jog with it and retain control and possession of it if you're blitzed (attacked from behind and don't see it coming) or scared. When you are surprised, your hand will automatically open. Having it wrapped around your hand will prevent you from dropping the device when you need it most, during an attack.
- I prefer one with a flashlight attachment and a GPS alert system.

- Purchase several practice canisters so you can learn how to use them to maximum effect.

I recommend the Tigerlight D.A.D. (Defense Alert Device; www.tiger light.net). It's an all-in-one tool with a strap so you won't drop it and comes with a belt holster. Even better, it doesn't look like your average pepper spray. It resembles a cell phone.

Pros:

- Compact
- Highly effective when used with the element of surprise
- Legal in all fifty states

Cons:

- Useless if it is at the bottom of your pocketbook or backpack
- Smaller canisters, not mentioned here, can be difficult to manage in your hand
- Must remember to replace the canister every couple of years
- Some states do not allow you to purchase pepper spray devices online

Taser/Stun Gun

The Taser and other stun devices are available, but not legal, in all states. Check your local laws before attempting to purchase or bring a stun gun home. When I became a Taser instructor, I was shot in the back with two darts. The 50,000-volt device immediately brought me down. It was the most intense pain I have ever experienced.

The Taser civilian model suggests that when you drop the device, it will continue to operate for thirty seconds, allowing you to escape. If you file a police report, the company will replace the device you left behind at no cost. The Taser is an effective device, but you will have to keep the batteries charged and be accurate when firing the darts. If they miss the intended target, or if the subject is wearing thick or loose-fitting clothing, you may not be able to create an effective electric circuit.

It is not to be confused with small handheld devices that require you to touch a predator's body with the electric contacts.

Pros:

- Highly effective when used properly

Cons:

- Expensive
- Not legal in all states
- Battery must be charged
- Both darts must hit the predator's body

Knives

I went from carrying a Spyderco folding knife that can be opened with one hand to a smaller and lighter Ka-Bar fixed-blade law enforcement knife. While I never used it as a defensive weapon, I taught law enforcement a knife-cutting defense technique, to be used as a last resort, if they were blitzed and caught in a rear choke.

A good number of my female instructors carry one or more knives as a defensive weapon, but they are highly trained in how to use them and they practice on a regular basis. They are also familiar with the laws that govern use of force. If you choose to carry a knife, seek out the best training possible. The Indonesian and Filipino arts have some amazing programs, just to name a couple.

Pros:

- Highly effective with proper training

Cons:

- Cross-contamination of blood-borne pathogens
- Require a great deal of training

- Can cause serious physical injury or death
- Must be justified in resorting to high level use of force against another person

Guns

Regardless of whether you choose to carry a concealed handgun or purchase a shotgun for home safety, it is a big responsibility and safety is of the utmost concern. While gun laws vary from state to state, I'm a huge advocate of training. Good training leads to responsibility, safety, and efficiency with any weapon, and especially with a gun. If you choose to carry a firearm, I recommend going to a range regularly and staying up to date with the best training you can find. I have used a variety of force simulators and recently demoed a Ti Simulator at my favorite indoor gun range.* The Ti Simulator creates reality-based shoot/don't-shoot scenarios. The simulator operator can create scenarios based upon your actions, reactions, and commands. It's very interactive and a great learning tool.

The simulator uses real weapons converted to operate under CO_2 pressure, and the 9mm Glock simulator weapon I use gives 65 percent simulated recoil of a real weapon. The Ti Simulator can also create low-light scenarios and you can train with pepper spray, flashlights, and a baton. Before using or procuring a gun, you should learn about the use-of-force laws for your state and region and in what situations you would choose to use a firearm for self-defense.

No weapon can replace your common sense or adhering to your intuitive self.

Other Improvised Weapons

CELL PHONE. Most people are attached to their cell phones. You always have it in your hand or accessible and it can be used as an early alert or to notify someone that you have encountered trouble.

---

* Blue Line Tactical is the type of range you should find to practice in. They offer safety classes, use-of-force classes, a simulator, everything you need to learn best practices and stay safe. See www.bluelinetactical.com.

TEN DOLLARS OF QUARTERS IN A SOCK. Double up two heavy-duty socks and pour a roll of quarters in. You now have an effective blunt instrument. I have found when pressure testing that a single sock will break after just a few strikes.

BACKPACK. Can be used to strike another person as well as to keep a barrier between you and a predator.

UMBRELLA. A large, sturdy umbrella with a hardwood handle can be used as a blunt instrument.

Other possible weapons

- A walking stick or cane
- A heavy buckle belt

Noise Devices

Anything that attracts the attention of people and alerts them to a possible problem is a good thing. However, you can never rely on someone coming to your defense. The good thing is that the predator doesn't know that and fears getting caught and getting hurt.

Some of the rescue whistles used by boaters and hunters can be heard for miles. They are extremely loud, but if you blow into them too hard, they do not work very well. During a time of panic and crisis, you will have trouble modulating your breath. Another consideration if you are thinking about using a sound device is that we, as a society, have become desensitized to alarms. While alarms are more reliable today than they were twenty years ago, there are an overwhelming number of false alarms in comparison to real-life emergencies.

Pros:

- Can attract attention and alert those around you to a potential threat

Cons:

- Have to be within reach when trouble starts, and not at the bottom of your backpack or purse

- Society is desensitized to alarms and sound devices
- You can't count on someone coming to your assistance

GPS Alert Devices

There are nearly five thousand GPS apps available for download onto your smartphone. Most of them have the ability to alert your friends and/or the police. Some apps provide your designated contacts with the police department number you should call based on your GPS location. Once the alert is activated, some apps will take photos or video of your surroundings.

On some apps, the service will first attempt to call you before calling the police. If you fail to answer within a specific time period, they dial the police. While this is a useful feature, there is an estimated loss of response time of about five to seven minutes.

Some of the apps have a "make a call to yourself" feature, which I believe is very valuable and that alone makes it worth purchasing the app. You can schedule phone calls to yourself at different time intervals and you can even give a false caller ID. For instance, if you have a contractor coming over, you could schedule a call from your "boyfriend" ten minutes after the contractor's arrival and another one fifteen minutes later from your "mother."

Pros:

- When activated, will alert your emergency notification list
- Have a "call police" function that will activate on some devices when your finger is removed; PIN code needed to disable the alerts

Cons:

- Time gap between activation of the alert and notification of the police
- May not always send the alert to the correct police department

Pressure Testing

No matter what your choice is for a personal defense device, you will need to test it and your skills under pressure. For example, if you carry a weapon of any kind on your waist or in an accessible area of your pocketbook or backpack, you need to pressure-test it by drawing it from under your blouse or shirt, in your car, with a coat on. There are also some very concealing holders and holsters available.

Start slowly and deliberately. Speed will come later. Once you are familiar with the tool, add in visualization under a variety of situations. See yourself in the moment. If practicing with a handgun, ensure the gun is unloaded during the pressure-testing session.

For example, you are walking to your car one night, going home later than expected. You spot someone off to the side of your direct route to the car. Ask yourself, "How do I feel right now? How is my body reacting to the potential threat?" You detect a little swirl in your belly and your senses are telling you this just doesn't look right. You reach for the side pocket of your backpack, just as you have done a hundred times, to take out your pepper spray. It happens to be the kind you can wrap around your hand so as not to drop it if things get serious. It's in your hand in a second, just like you practiced. If it was at the bottom of your bag, you would be done. You are searching in your mind for the blueprint you have made and added to over time. You need only a couple of seconds to review. You go from a yellow state of alert to orange and ready to advance if necessary. Suddenly he steps off to your right and you don't see him anymore. Your car is still a distance away and you have your keys in your free hand. But you don't want to unlock the car and give away your destination. You were walking in a straight line and now you decide to walk slightly left, in the opposite direction of where you last saw him.

You walk a bit farther and do a tactical pause, utilizing all of your senses to take in your environment. You hear a slight noise off to your right side. It has to be him. You scan as you start walking to your car. Here he comes. He's lost the element of surprise and you don't let him know that you have the pepper spray in your hand. The element of surprise with pepper spray works to your advantage every time.

As he gets close, blast him with the pepper spray. Then take a couple of steps to the side because he knows where you were last. He's going to be on fire with police-grade pepper spray but he may still come after you.

When you depressed the pepper spray, the device sent an alert to your designated contacts that you are at work (gives GPS location). You run to your car, which you have backed in, for a fast retreat, and you drive out. Before you are out of the lot, your dad calls, frantic, and asks if you are okay. "No," you say, and ask him to call the *Anywhere USA Police Department*. You will also call them; it's listed in your favorite places. You give your name and say, "I was attacked in the parking lot of *123 Main Street, Anywhere, USA.*" You describe what the attacker was wearing and let them know that you sprayed him with pepper spray. He won't be able to get far and he certainly will not be able to drive after exposure to the spray. It's likely he will be caught. The police will advise you what to do next.

A blueprint like this should take less than a minute to review once you have the original plan in your head.

TAKEAWAYS

- Your brain is your most powerful weapon.
- Not being familiar with self-defense at this close range is unforgiving.
- Fight smart. Use your most powerful physical weapons against his vulnerable points.

8
THE DIGITAL ENVIRONMENT

You Don't Know What You Don't Know About Social Media

The information contained in this chapter is important for both parents and young adults. For parents, it gets right to the point of how advanced and sophisticated children are with their devices and in managing social media. We need to have a proactive parenting mindset and learn about the power and potential dangers of the online world, a place where anonymous adults can befriend minors, under the radar and with no supervision. Later in the chapter we will touch upon safety for young adults, particularly females, when using social media, especially for socializing and dating.

The digital world is fascinating and has opened new ways of connecting and communicating. It can be used for so many things: to meet people, to buy and sell goods and services, to market your business, for education. Its reach is endless. In each of these arenas, there is much positive, but we are heading into a world of advanced technology without the education to keep us safe. We are ten to fifteen years behind the curve in teaching our youth, and especially young women, about how to stay safe online.

Sergeant Marty Greenberg has been a detective in the youth division at the Mount Pleasant, New York, police department since social media started in the late 1990s.

He says, "It began with the creation of AOL chat rooms and the fact that children learned to navigate the Internet much faster than their parents. The same is true today . . . children and teenagers are not just a step ahead of adults—they are miles ahead. Kids feel invincible. When apps become boring, a new flavor of the week is created. Even stories about kids who learn the hard way that whatever you post stays forever (threats, naked photos) don't stop it from continuing to happen to other teens. No one believes it will ever happen to them."

Millennials are comfortable and highly competent with technology. Generation Zs are naturals online and interact on social media for a significant amount of their socializing. It's as if they were born with a mobile device in their hands. What takes an adult an hour to figure out on a smartphone will be solved by a kid in minutes. Want to learn about the coolest apps? The latest in social media? Just ask your kid.

Technology and social media have changed rapidly over the years and so have the safety measures we need to put into place. In the past, the advice from law enforcement and educators was to keep the computer in the area where your carpet was most worn—so that the screen and, most important, what was on it could be seen and accessed by everyone. But today, the big bulky desktop fits into the palm of your hand.

With the advent of Wi-Fi, the recommendation was for parents to limit accessibility or data. Now the suggestion is that you become familiar with contemporary mobile devices and social media apps. You wouldn't give your daughter the keys to your car without first teaching her how to drive. Yet we hand over eight-hundred-dollar smartphones to our kids without teaching them the basics about online safety.

It goes without saying that:

- Teens will create two accounts: one for you and one for their friends.

- There are apps that will allow your teen to hide and password-protect pictures, videos, and documents.

- Many social media accounts will allow anyone aged thirteen or older to sign up and there is often no verification process. Only a date of birth is required and that is rarely verified.

- Kids are going to make mistakes.

As time passes, it is becoming apparent that smartphones are being used as babysitters. Parents have trouble keeping up with the advancements in technology and are not teaching the principles of digital citizenship within their homes.

Schools are overwhelmed with sexting and cyber-harassment, and in the limited time they have, they don't teach students how to use these tools. They push the use of technology in the classrooms, give out laptops under pressure from families, and wait for parents to supervise and manage.

The Rule of Five

The Rule of Five is the principle that you should start discussing an issue with your child five years in advance of when they will have to deal with it. This is particularly true for sex, alcohol, the Internet, dating, drugs, or self-defense.

The conversation will be developmentally appropriate for a child's age. A conversation with an eight-year-old will be very different from one with a twelve-year-old or even with a sixteen-year-old.

Experts in the field, like Katey McPherson, executive director of the Gurian Institute (www.gurianinstitute.com), frame the discussion like this: "Do you want to provide your children with the answers to their questions or would you rather they learn them from the Internet or other kids?"

The approach is never simple. You need to first understand what your kids know, because you don't want to give them more than they need and you want to remain within an age-appropriate discussion.

Social Media Is "Prey" Grounds for the Predator

■■■

Many apps create a forum where there is no oversight or monitoring of relationships. Adults can befriend minors, allowing potential predators to have contact with underage children and develop relationships with them. Without your knowledge and without understanding by the child, a predator will surreptitiously groom them for future contact. Issues such as cyberbullying are also a problem.

GROOMING

A sexual predator engages in grooming when the predator gains access to a child by any means necessary. The predator then builds a relationship with the child and gets the child to trust him. The predator may be known or unknown to the child's family and friends.

The popularity of apps changes constantly and a list of the "in" ones would probably be outdated by the time you finish this book. Below is a list of app concepts and what every parent should be aware of:

Hookup Apps

These are apps used for hooking up and dating. Users find a potential hookup via a GPS location tracking. Sites like this often have a rating system, and millions of profiles are rated daily. The safer apps use Facebook to authenticate.

DANGERS: It's easy for adults and minors to locate one another. Rating systems can be used for bullying when kids target or group-target other kids, causing their rating to go down.

Photo-Video Apps that Disappear

These apps allow a user to send photos and videos to anyone on their friends list. The sender can set a time limit for viewing the image and it will disappear once the time expires.

DANGERS: These apps are at the top of the list for sexting because people believe that it is a safe way to sext. The photos can easily be recovered and the person receiving the image or video can do a screenshot, enabling the images to possibly be used for revenge porn.

Flirting Apps

Flirting apps are used to meet people through GPS location services. You can send photos, videos, and messages and many of these apps have rating systems.

DANGERS: No authentication requirement. Predators can contact and set up meetings with minors. Promotes sexting and the rating system can be used to attack a child or teen.

Instant-Messaging Apps

Apps allow users to exchange photos, videos, and sketches. Users can exchange YouTube videos, digital gifts, and memes.

DANGERS: Kids/teens can use these apps for sexting and sending nude selfies. Username can be used to place classified ads for sex on other sites. For example, a bag of weed might be offered for a sexual favor. An easy way for sexual predators to interact and hook up with minors. There is no authentication and no parental controls.

Anonymous-Confession Apps

Allows users to superimpose text over an image to express their thoughts/feelings anonymously. Yes, the posting is anonymous but it sends out a GPS location. GPS will give other users a precise location of the user.

DANGERS: App is anonymous and kids can post photos of others with defamatory texting posted over the image. Users do not have to register and can communicate with others close by via GPS. You can see what others are writing but you don't know their identity. Predators can use to locate children or teens and attempt to establish a relationship.

Question-and-Answer Apps

Mostly used by kids and teens. Sites like this allow users to ask questions while remaining anonymous.

DANGER: This is an anonymous site and allows for the targeting of individuals by others, much like an Internet wolf-pack mentality.

Text-Only Apps

App allows users to post a limited number of characters. Posts can be viewed by hundreds of posters who are closest to the poster as determined by GPS tracking.

DANGERS: As with other anonymous sites, the posters will reveal personal information. Content on text-only sites is usually sexually explicit, defamatory, and includes personal attacks.

Hidden Apps

Apps your kids don't want you to know about and are hidden from view.

DANGER: These apps are constantly being created and used by children and teens to hide their social media activity.

Video-Chatting Apps

Primarily used for video chatting. You can connect these apps to your Facebook account to locate and chat with strangers who have similar interests via your likes.

DANGER: Predators can use it to collect personal information and then have the ability to track or meet someone in person or stalk them.

Hookup Apps for Facebook

Users can categorize their Facebook friends into two categories: people they would like to hang with or people they would like to hook up with sexually.

DANGERS: Can create a false impression that you want to have sex with a particular friend or that the user may think the friend is hot. As with any classification system, people will feel left out and resentful. Many of the users are under the age of consent for sexual activity.

Staying Safe Online

There are many privacy settings that you can set so that you can stay safe online. From software to hardware, programs installed on your devices, and the old-fashioned art of just being smart, you can stay safe.

Most social media platforms have privacy settings that allow you to only share your information with a select group of friends, colleagues, and partners. The challenge for young people is that the more likes and followers you have, the more dopamine (the feel-good chemical) is dumped into the brain. Dopamine makes you feel good. You can get it in lots of places, including video games, apps, and likes. This is why mobile phones are addictive.

The following are examples of software, online apps, programs, and websites that provide practical and up-to-date information on the digital landscape for parents as well as young adults:

OurPact
Circle with Disney
Net Nanny
TeenSafe
Spector Pro
NetSmartz
FBI.gov

Think Before You Post

Before you post any personal information on the Internet, ask yourself, "What do I want the world to know about me?" The less information that is out there, the less likely you are to run into trouble. Information is the source of a criminal's action. The more of it there is, the better for someone wishing to do you harm. Whenever you have personal information online, you are a target for attackers. They go after the low-hanging fruit, so it is very important to make yourself a hard target online.

You, as an Avatar

When you use social media online, create an avatar or double agent, who represents the public you without giving away too much personal information. The focus of your avatar needs to be secure, through platform privacy settings; safe, by being educated on the hidden, lurking dangers; and strategic, meaning it can still promote and brand your personality, likes, and dislikes, just safely.

Consider the following whenever you post anything online:

- What images are you sharing?

- Does your profile picture on any platform give away specific information about you?

- Does it showcase your attributes, or does it showcase a different message that could be misread and put you in potential danger?

- Does it give away personally identifying information about where you live, work, go to school? Does your clothing have your school logo on it?

- Do you personally know the people you are talking to and messaging online, or are you trusting it is the person in the photo?

Online Dating

Melissa, a twenty-five-year-old student from California, had not dated for two years. She had been consumed with pursuing a master's degree in social work and working full-time. As her program drew to a close, she decided to venture back into the dating world. Melissa was tired of the bar scene and getting set up on dates. She decided to try online dating and she created a profile on a popular dating site. A romantic at heart, she was excited to see whom she would meet.

She soon met Ken, a twenty-six-year-old who worked in sales and lived about thirty minutes from where she worked. His profile picture showed a clean-cut male wearing a well-pressed military uniform, the second picture showed him with his family and a dog, and in the third one he was with his sister's baby. They wrote back and forth for a week and eventually spoke on the phone. A few days later, Melissa agreed to meet Ken at his apartment. She did not tell any of her friends or family what she was doing or where she was going.

Five weeks later, the police found Melissa's body. It was buried in a shallow grave in the desert.

Ken had never been in the military. Ken did not work in sales. Ken was not clean-cut. His body was covered in gang tattoos, which he had hidden in his profile photo, and he had an extensive criminal history. He had lured Melissa to his apartment through his fake online profile and brutally killed her. Ken was a fraud and may have been catfishing. A "catfish" is a person who creates a false online identity in the hopes of tricking people into romantic relationships, particularly to pursue deceptive activities.

With over $1 billion in annual revenue, the online dating industry is big business. More than 50 million people in the United States have used online dating sites. Digital technology and smartphones, in particular, have radically transformed many aspects of our society, including how people seek out and establish romantic relationships.

When the Pew Research Center first polled on online dating in 2005, few Americans had experience with the activity. Today, 15 percent of U.S. adults report they have used online dating sites or mobile dating apps. The share of 18-to-24-year-olds who use online dating has roughly tripled from 10 percent in 2013 to 27 percent today. One factor behind the substantial growth among younger adults is their use of mobile dating apps. About one in five 18-to-24-year-olds (22 percent) now report using dating apps; in 2013, only 5 percent reported doing so.*

Among the 25–34 age group, one in five are using at least one of the popular dating sites.

Michael DeBiase, a Certified Information Systems Security Professional (CISSP), recommends trying to meet someone IRL (in real life) at your local coffee shop, neighborhood bar, church, gym, or bookstore.

However, if you are going to date online, I suggest using a paid service. The more expensive the website, the better the chance that the person is not faking who they are. Free websites like plentyoffish.com or Craigslist are the worst for catfishing. Also, be wary of mobile dating apps, since they track your location. Make sure you turn this feature off.

---

* Pew Internet Research Study, February 11, 2016.

DeBiase also says that every time you take a picture on your cell, it records not only the date, but also the location where it was taken. This is a geotag and it is stored inside the image. Remove all geotagging from photos you take on a cell phone before posting anywhere online, especially on dating sites. Stalkers and hackers are always looking for geotags. It has never been easier for people with bad intentions to gather personal data about you. This could include things like pictures of you and family members, information about restaurants and bars you frequent on a regular basis, your home address, or your work address. Without being careful, any time you post on social media you are giving away valuable information about your activities and whereabouts.

Be on the Lookout for Red Flags

When you meet someone online, be cautious. If you sense something does not feel right, abandon your contact with that person, or at the very least, proceed slowly. While the purpose of joining an online dating site is to meet new people, your personal safety is always the priority. It is not rude or a sign that you don't trust people to take things slowly. Anyone who says that to you does not deserve your trust. Do not give the benefit of the doubt to a total stranger.

- Run a general Internet search of his name and see what comes up. If his picture appears on various other sites or comes up under a different name, it is not a good sign.

- Take it slow. Talk for a few days online or on the site before exchanging email addresses or cell numbers. Consider creating an email account specific for online dating. This account should not reveal your full name. Anyone rushing you for any reason should be considered suspect.

- If he immediately asks you to chat with him off the site, using personal email or another messaging service, be very careful.

- If he can't send you a picture instantly or doesn't have access to a webcam, that is a red flag. He might not want you to know who he is or he might not even look like you would expect.

- If he asks for money or wants you to send him a package, that is a red flag.

- If he has excessive grammar and spelling errors and does not have a great working knowledge of the language, that is a red flag.

- If he asks for your address so he can send a gift or flowers, do not give it to him. Not even your work address or your best friend's address or your mother's address.

Play Detective and Test Their Honesty

The advantage of meeting someone in person is that you can consciously and subconsciously evaluate them. You read their body language and get an overall impression. Do they seem stable? Do they seem honest? Do they seem shifty? It is much harder to form an opinion exchanging only emails. When you ask questions online, you are looking for a trail of integrity, which is easier to feel out when you are sharing dinner in person.

- Ask a question, and then later ask the same question in a different way. You might ask him about his family, where he grew up, or even seemingly mundane things such as his favorite color or the type of car he drives. If he gives you inconsistent answers, be alert.

- If he avoids answering your questions, especially about issues that are important to you, be alert. It's okay if people joke about their answer, but eventually they need to get around to responding to the question or explaining why they feel uncomfortable doing so.

- If he makes disrespectful comments about you or other people, be alert. How your match treats others can be a telling sign into their future behavior.

- If he has inconsistencies about any basic information, especially anything within his profile, be alert. This especially includes marital status, children, employment, and where he is living, but also things such as age, appearance, education, and career.

Stalking

After three years in an abusive relationship with a man named Peter, Monica finally left him. Shortly after that, he began stalking her. Initially he called her repeatedly on her phone, he followed her, he waited in the bushes for her at work. Over time, he began putting up profanity-laced posters with Monica's phone number at her work and other locations she frequented. It continued to get worse. He began harassing her mom and her new boyfriend, allegedly setting fire to the boyfriend's house.

Monica moved to a different state, but Peter was relentless. He posed as a police officer and discovered the name of her moving company. The moving company, however, refused to release her new address. Then he posed as a private investigator and was able to find where she lived. He flew back and forth several times, casing her new neighborhood. Eventually he located a UPS driver and convinced him to reveal her new address. The next morning, Peter broke into her new home, where he killed her and then killed himself.

Monica did everything right. She took all the right steps to attempt to leave him. She had people at work and her friends and neighbors watching out for her and she obtained an order of protection. She even moved several states away to conceal her new identity and her new home. Peter was determined to find her and, sadly, he did.

How Much Do You Know About Stalking?

Take this brief quiz* and see how much you know about stalking. The statistics are provided by the Department of Justice and the Centers for Disease Control and Prevention. The correct answers are at the end of the quiz.

1. How many people are stalked in the United States each year?
    A. 850,000
    B. 3.4 million
    C. 5 million
    D. 7.5 million

2. How many states have stalking laws?
    A. 24
    B. 34
    C. 48
    D. 50

* Quiz taken from the Stalking Resource Center of the National Center for Victims of Crime.

3. Most stalking victims are stalked by strangers.
   A. True
   B. False

4. Most stalking victims report stalking to the police.
   A. True
   B. False

5. Which age group has the highest victimization?
   A. 18–24
   B. 25–34
   C. 35–49
   D. 50–64

6. Most stalking victims are stalked by current or former intimate partners.
   A. True
   B. False

7. Which one of the following is common stalking behavior?
   A. Following
   B. Frequent phone calls
   C. Monitoring computer usage
   D. All of the above

8. Ignore a stalker and he will go away.
   A. True
   B. False

9. Most stalkers are mentally ill.
   A. True
   B. False

10. Technology is used by only the savviest stalkers.
    A. True
    B. False

Answers

1. D—The Centers for Disease Control and Prevention report that 7.5 million people were stalked in one year.

2. D—Stalking is a crime in all fifty states, the District of Columbia, and most U.S. territories.

3. False—Most stalking victims are stalked by someone they know.

4. False—Only 41 percent of stalking victims report the crime to police. Victims choose not to report for a variety of reasons, including minimizing the seriousness of what they are experiencing, not understanding that the behavior is criminal, and thinking that the police won't take it seriously.

5. A—The 18–24 age group has the highest incidence of victimization. As with victimization risk more generally, risk of being stalked diminishes with age.

6. True—61 percent of women report being stalked by current and former intimate partners.

7. D—All of the above. Stalkers use a variety of methods to monitor, harass, and threaten their targets.

8. False—Stalkers rarely go away and their stalking behavior may escalate over time, even if the woman ignores them.

9. False—Although studies show that some stalkers suffer from mental illness, there is no evidence that most stalkers are mentally ill.

10. False—Increasingly, stalkers use readily available and easy-to-use technologies (such as cell phones, computers, email, cameras, video

devices, and GPS monitoring) to track their targets. More than one in four stalking victims report that some type of technology was used.

In 2007, there were 1.1 million reported stalkings. Today the number has jumped to 7.5 million. Social media and the digital environment have made this possible. We are not matching our safety with today's technology.

Stalkers are very unpredictable. Typical behavior includes threats, physical assaults, sexual assaults, destruction of property, online and phone harassment, and harassment of friends, family, and coworkers. In extreme cases, there are fatalities. Sadly, there is no single behavioral profile that can predict what a stalker might do next.

Many stalking victims don't know or understand what action is appropriate to stop the stalker from making life miserable. Often, before a woman goes to the police or to an outside support agency such as victims' assistance, a family court, or a women's shelter, she will attempt to reason with the stalker, minimize his behavior, and believe it will get better over time. Some women will threaten, or have the stalker threatened, by a third party. I was working with a woman who had been raped by her ex-husband; the rapist served ten years in prison and was about to be released. Her current husband had some powerful ties and was planning on sending some rough-and-tough people to have some choice words with him upon his release. He asked for my opinion and I asked him to consider the following:

Will he be intimidated by the threats and leave your family alone? Or will he see it as an affront and challenge and perhaps retaliate against your family? (What do you think? He elected not to do anything.)

When a woman recognizes that she has become the subject of unwanted attention, she needs to immediately begin creating a blueprint for a plan of action for what to do if she runs into the stalker at home, work, the gym, school, a friend's house, or a place where she socializes. This should include anywhere she frequently travels, especially places the stalker knows about. She must develop the habit of checking the back seat of her car and scanning the area before she leaves any of these places. She has to ask herself, "Does he have keys to my house or car?" If so, she should have the locks changed.

Behavior doesn't lie. If you believe you are being stalked, it is very likely that you are. Listen to your gut. Stop and think about how this person makes you feel and how your senses are reacting to him.

Protect Your Computer

If the stalker has access to your computer, your history can be tracked and any websites you have visited will be revealed. On a daily basis, clear your history off your computer. Stalkers who have access to your computer could also install spyware. This can be done by manually installing a program, or it can be sent through a corrupt email. If your computer has been compromised, every keystroke made, including passwords, websites you have visited, and emails you have sent, can be tracked.

Using the Internet to Harass and Assault Your Character

The stalker can use the Internet to contact people you know or post about you on public message boards. He can also create blogs, writing messages or stories that assault your character. Many blog hosts will remove bogus or slanderous posts from their site if you legally request removal of the page and submit a complaint or have an attorney submit a cease-and-desist letter. Other sites are more difficult and will require action by the court. This can be time-consuming and costly.

The allegations that rise to the level of defamation or slander are actionable. It varies by state, but typically the statute of limitations can run from six months to up to three years to bring action.

Mobile Apps

Facebook, Twitter, dating apps, health apps that count how many steps you have taken—all can track your whereabouts. Most of the apps on your mobile device can track your location. Google, Google Maps, and Amazon can track where you have been, what you purchased, and what you were shopping for. We, as mobile device owners, cannot keep up with technology, and neither can law enforcement. Turning off the location service setting on your phone will help prevent some of the tracking, but nothing can guarantee that you are not being tracked. Everything from Fitbits to baby cameras are hooked up online. All these devices can be hacked and used by stalkers to track you.

Sextortion

Brooke, a young beauty queen, received an anonymous email containing a series of private and personal photographs of her. Along with the photos was a letter from the extortionist, demanding that she send better-quality sexually explicit photos and get on Snapchat or get on Skype with him for five minutes and do whatever he asked. He threatened her by saying that if she did not fulfill one of the three demands, he would make her private photos public and ruin her career. Every day she received dozens of emails, threatening her and attempting to blackmail her.

A hacker had taken over her computer's webcam and secretly spent a year recording her getting ready for school in the morning and getting undressed at night. He had remotely installed spyware commonly referred to as "creepware." Feeling violated and helpless, she eventually went to the police, who involved the FBI. The hacker was arrested and charged in federal court. You can combat this with a simple piece of tape placed over your webcam.

A similar incident occurred at a school in Virginia, where a suspect gained the trust of two college students and enticed them to broadcast their sexual acts on their webcam. The suspect recorded the acts and threatened that he would post the videos on the Internet unless they paid five thousand dollars. The incidents were reported to the authorities and the university released a bulletin warning students to beware.

This relatively new crime is called sextortion, the threat to release sexually explicit photographs or videos in exchange for money or more sexual content, including photos and videos. Usually young girls and women are targeted. They are manipulated into giving in to the extortionist's demands because they are afraid they will be punished by their parents for doing something wrong in the first place. Women may go along in the belief that the sextortion will stop once they fulfill a request, but the demand for more sexual content or money doesn't end that easily.

The FBI is calling it a significant and global threat, again stressing that the vast majority of targets are younger female teens. In one case, a twenty-six-year-old Florida man victimized more than 350 young girls on social media and chat sites in twenty-six states, three Canadian provinces, and the United Kingdom. The suspect would target girls through social networking sites and pretend to be an acquaintance, a friend, or an admirer, according to the FBI. Once he gained their trust, he would persuade the girls to expose themselves or engage in sexually explicit conduct on video chats. He then threatened to put the images online or send them to the girls' parents unless they agreed to provide more graphic images.

The suspect told authorities that he targeted girls who ranged in age from thirteen to eighteen because adults were "too smart" to fall for his scheme. Using screen names like Captain Obvious, Tyler the Conqueror, and HotGuy160112, he posed as a sixteen-year-old boy who was interested in skateboarding and his profile photo showed a blond kid at the beach. The suspect collected more than eighty thousand pictures and videos that he used to threaten his victims, warning them he would hurt them or their families. He used multiple proxy servers that hid his identity, routing his communications through other countries. He was sentenced to 105 years in prison, after pleading guilty in federal court to nine counts of producing child pornography. Many of his victims have yet to be identified.

This is problematic for law enforcement because these suspects are hard to trace and frequently operate in another country. The targets often suffer from severe emotional trauma and some have committed or attempted suicide. Law enforcement sees this as one of the greatest threats to young women in the digital age.

Revenge Porn

Revenge porn is the distribution of one or more sexually explicit photos of someone without the subject's permission. The photo may be one that the victim took herself and shared with the poster, or it may be a photo taken by someone else (usually an ex-boyfriend, husband, or lover). It could also be an image taken from the victim's computer by a hacker. The victims are almost always female. The damage done to their reputations and the resulting mental anguish are tremendous.

In the United States about two-thirds of the states have passed laws addressing revenge porn. Victims in states that do not have such laws rely on a variety of related laws to prosecute the predator, if at all. Federal legislation has been discussed and will likely be implemented in the future. A civil suit in which a victim would go after a predator for monetary damages is also an option.

Revenge Porn Sites

Revenge porn sites feature nude and sexual photos mostly of women, often posted by their ex-spouses or ex-boyfriends. A number of websites host these images and many sites include personal information, such as the woman's name, employer, and where she lives. Some will include links to the person's social media or other personal Web pages. Many revenge porn sites have been successfully shut down but others pop up just as fast. Images can be picked up by other websites, and content that is widely distributed on the Internet is often difficult to remove completely.

Unlawful Surveillance

With the development of tiny cameras that can be concealed in almost anything (see list below), women in particular run the risk of being unlawfully captured in their most intimate moments. The statutory wording varies, but it is a crime in all fifty states if you install a device that records, broadcasts, or permits you to view images of a person without their consent. You may face serious charges. This includes locations where privacy is expected, such as a changing room, bedroom, bathroom, toilet, shower, or any place that people will be dressing and undressing and have a reasonable expectation of privacy. This crime also occurs in hotels, motels, and inns.

10 Common Video Surveillance Devices

- USB flash drives
- Men's shower gel
- Wi-Fi plug-in adapter
- Electrical outlet
- Tissue box
- Toilet brush spy cam
- Smoke detector
- Alarm clock
- Cell phone charger
- Footwear camera

A simple way to spot most types of cameras is to look for the lens reflection. This requires turning off the lights and slowly scanning the room with a flashlight. You are looking for bright reflections. Be sure to scan the room from multiple spots so you don't miss a camera pointed only at a certain place. Also, do a close inspection of vents as well as any holes or gaps in the walls or ceilings.

There are security companies that sell hidden camera detectors, lens detectors, and radio frequency detectors for devices that transmit radio signals. Prices range from less than $100 up to $1,000. Close inspection of electronic devices that you find in a bedroom or bathroom is your best defense.

What You Post Now Can Hurt You Later

Retired Arizona trooper and safety expert Laurie Latham is an investigative consultant for the National Football League and the Indoor Football League (formerly the Arena Football League), examining players, cheerleaders, and other prospective employees. As a part of the investigative process, Laurie does open-source searches on social media. Negative social media posts or embarrassing posts and photos have completely eliminated many otherwise highly qualified candidates.

The biggest story for the NFL draft for 2016 was early-round prospect Laremy Tunsil and the now-infamous Twitter video of him wearing a gas mask and smoking a substance from a bong. The video was posted to his Twitter account thirteen minutes before the start of the NFL draft. It was deleted immediately but the damage was done.

According to Fortune Sports, his estimated monetary loss was between $8 million and $13 million.

Ransomware

Cybercriminals will infect your computer with malicious code and your files and data will be encrypted. The only way for you to access them is to pay a ransom. You will be given instructions on what to do, which usually involves changing currency into bitcoins or other crypto-currency that cannot be traced. There will likely be a warning that if the ransom is not paid, it will double. Businesses, corporations, and private citizens are targeted.

Experts estimate that ransomware costs the consumer billions of dollars a year and they expect that to double by 2021. Keep all your software up to date, back up your computer daily, and follow the basics on being a hard target online, as listed below.

10 Ways to Be a Hard Target Online*

1. Do not click on links within email messages. Email phishing scams are on the rise, but you can avoid them by not clicking on the link. The email may address you by name. For example, it will say, "Hey, Steve, have you seen this amazing product here?" or it will give just a simple "Hi!"

2. If you are going to buy things online, make sure you are using a credit card that you only use online. Also, make sure you keep track of the statements for that card. If there is a fraudulent purchase made, it will be easier to figure out that the card was compromised online. Watch for small unauthorized purchases online. They are tests to see if you are monitoring your account for larger fraudulent purchases later.

* Credit: Michael DeBiase.

3. When you aren't using your webcam, keep it covered with tape. A hacker, even an amateur, can easily compromise your webcam and begin watching you remotely.

4. Use antivirus and anti-malware software on your computer. Running basic antivirus and anti-malware scans should keep many threats off your computer.

5. Never use the same password twice. If you are using the same password all over the place, a hacker can obtain access to many of your accounts with a single exploit.

6. Use random passphrases instead of passwords. For example, instead of using a password like *Ye110wCar2017* you are better off using random words such as *pepperonibasketballscissorsmagenta*. The latter is harder for a computer to crack but easier for a human to remember. The longer the string of words, the better.

7. Set up two-factor authentication on accounts that offer it. Many companies, such as Yahoo and Google, now offer two-factor authentication for free. This usually involves either a token sent to you via text message and a password, or a fingerprint scan or facial scan and a password. Using more than one factor creates a lot of work for a hacker.

8. Never use public Wi-Fi. It is very easy for attackers to sit at the local public Wi-Fi spots and listen to all the data traveling on the network. You may think that person at the coffee shop is just browsing the Web, but they may be trying to intercept your conversations, images, and bank info.

9. Only visit websites that start with "https," especially if you are going to enter personal info. Anything sent without "https" is sent in plain text and is easily intercepted by an attacker. Also, not having an https website signifies that you aren't serious about security.

10. Only share videos/photos/messages that you wouldn't mind the public seeing. If you send something online, do so knowing that there will be many eyes looking at it. It is very difficult to achieve pure confidentiality online.

Bonus tips: Be very careful with phone calls, since they are an easy way for an attacker to gain personal information about you. Never give out

Social Security numbers or other personal information to someone over the phone. The first step of every online attack is information gathering. If they don't have your information, they can't attack you.

The Dark Web

The dark web is an encrypted network that makes users anonymous and untraceable. Created by a navy research laboratory to protect U.S. intelligence online, it uses Tor servers and something known as the onion router.

Tor directs Internet traffic through a free, worldwide, volunteer network consisting of more than seven thousand relays to hide a user's location and usage from anyone conducting network surveillance or traffic analysis. Using Tor makes it difficult for Internet activity to be traced back to the user. This includes visits to websites, online posts, instant messages, and other communication forms.

The dark web is not discoverable by conventional means, such as a Google search or by directly entering a URL. It is a secret, underground marketplace where things such as drugs, guns, fake passports, child porn, or hit men can be bought anonymously. It has had an astounding effect on child pornography, whereby children in faraway, poverty-stricken countries are abused and viewed from anywhere in the world.

Federal law enforcement has had success in shutting down and persecuting dark web sites with names like Silk Road and Playpen.

TAKEAWAYS

- If you haven't met him in person, he is a stranger. No matter what you have shared or how long you have communicated, he is a stranger.

- All you know for sure about the person you're communicating with online is that he has access to a computer; nothing else, nothing more.

- While there are always ongoing investigations, stings, and investigators posing as potential victims, there is no such thing as Internet police to protect you.

- Keep a piece of tape over your computer camera and keep your webcam disconnected when not in use.

- Whatever you post online and on social media leaves a digital footprint. Regardless of what you do, it will be there and recoverable, forever.

ACKNOWLEDGMENTS

This book would have remained only a dream had it not been for my mentor and dear friend, Dr. Belisa Vranich, author of *Breathe*. Her guidance, direction, edits, and belief in me led me far outside my literary comfort zone to discover a new world in which I could spread the message of safety and empowerment to women of all ages.

A big thank-you to my literary agent, Peter McGuigan of Foundry Literary + Media, for seeing the great need for and value in this book from day one, and to Claire Harris and other members of the Foundry team who have worked behind the scenes on my behalf. The invaluable guidance and direction provided by my editor, Matthew Benjamin of Simon & Schuster, transformed my words into an essential and empowering guide. The tireless efforts of the Simon & Schuster team of Tara Parsons, Kelsey Manning, Shida A. Carr, and Lara Blackman have helped spread the word—thank you. A big thank-you also to my dedicated and amazing writer, A. Clara Pistek, who spent countless hours working with me on this book, polishing my words and thoughts.

Thanks to Brad Parker, for having the vision and creating the original program for Defend University, and for his support and contribution to women's safety. To my dear friend and trusted assistant, Carol Ann Williams, who has never waivered in her devotion to our mission. To Angela Rose, for her support and inspiration and devotion to sexual assault prevention. And to Elizabeth McCaffrey, who has assisted me locally since she was fourteen years old.

Thanks goes to the following for their invaluable contributions to this book: Renee Ellroy (Eyes for Lies), Laurie Latham, Katey McPherson, Tracie Alexander, Mike DeBiase, Marty Greenberg, Roger Canaff, Thong Nguyen, Ken Good, and David Regone for his amazing illustrations.

To my media family at *Inside Edition*, Bob Read, Megan Alexander, Diane McInerney, Les Trent, Deborah Norville, Charles Lachman, Lisa Guerrero, Jim Moret, Steven Fabian, Paul Boyd, and all the producers, cameramen, and support staff: a big thank-you for your years of support. And thank you to all my other friends in the media, including *Fox & Friends*' Ainsley Earhardt, Steve Doocy, Brian Kilmeade, Clayton Morris, Abby Huntsman, and Pete Hegseth. HLN/CNN *On the Story*'s Erica Hill, CNN and HLN producers Cameron Baird Markham, Tracey Jordan, and Carmen Conte Widman, and Sarah Carden, senior producer for the *Dr. Phil* show. Thank you all for helping me spread the good word of safety!

To my many friends, for the amazing support during the crunch to get this book completed, including but not limited to Mike Dolan, Mitch Gitter, Greg Porteus, Ed Kardian, Larry Orsini, and many others.

And a heartfelt thank-you to my martial arts instructors Phil Migliarese of Team Balance, and Erik Paulson and Tonya Paulson of Combat Submission Wrestling.

To my wife, Peg; my daughter, Kim; and my sons, Steve and John, for all of their love and support: You are my heroes.

ADDITIONAL RESOURCES

■■■■■■■■■■

Defend University

■■■

If you are interested in learning more strategies and practicing the self-defense moves shown in this book with an instructor, I welcome you to check out www.DefendUniversity.com and go to the instructor list.

During the past twenty years, we have reached an estimated 200,000 women and young girls. New techniques and risk-reduction strategies are added each year. This is *not* a martial arts program but rather a "women's-specific safety and self-defense program." A women's advocate with no martial arts training starts at the same basic level as a world champion martial artist.

How It Began

Defend University was founded more than twenty years ago by Brad Parker. In his experience, "One of the things that we see most often is empowerment of the women who go through the program. Having a method that allows you to effectively respond to full-power attacks from a male gives you confidence and knowledge. Being physically attacked in a controlled environment gives you the confidence that comes from actually solving your problem."

In the beginning, we taught women really good and effective martial arts moves. They worked well for us, and for women with previous martial arts training. But none of the non–martial artist women could:

- make the technique work within a time frame of thirty minutes; and
- remember the techniques at the end of the two-hour class when we went to review.

We realized that women needed self-defense moves that they could learn quickly, that felt natural, and that would be something they would retain during a stressful situation. The moves developed in Defend University were created over a period of seven years with hundreds of women, dealing with the most common sexual assault scenarios researched from real-life attacks and using survivors seeking effective answers to prevent the crimes that they had endured. The techniques were refined by using full-contact responses to full-power attacks from male role players, but we first taught the women basic techniques to a level of proficiency. We then combined some of the techniques and gradually added speed. The addition of a male role player wearing a padded suit took it to a new level. This is as close as it gets to a real-life attack. The women experienced the adrenaline rush, but they were familiar with the scenarios and the positions and were not frozen by fear, so they were able to fight back.

The Innovative Method

One of our innovations was to modify the program to start with the worst possible position you could find yourself in: the predator has you pinned down to the ground and is between your thighs.

Our system is organized in reverse of how most self-defense programs are taught. Normally they begin by teaching women how to avoid or evade the first contact and escalate from there. What to do if he grabs your wrist, then what to do if he grabs your shoulders, and so on.

Defend University starts with the sexual assault position and then goes backward, ending with maintaining your personal space. Avoidance and evasion are covered, but one of the core principles is that when you know you can always escape the worst position possible, the others are relatively simple by comparison.

Defend University does not depend very much on hitting. Although it is a favorite strategy of some well-publicized courses, the "stun and run" and "keep hitting him until he is down" philosophy plays right into the hands of the "fight like a man" game. If he is in the range of your hits, then you are in range of his. He will most likely be stronger than you, and he may be on drugs or enraged and running on adrenaline, which will make his hits all the more brutal.

Plus, you have to remember that men operate differently when fighting.

Ever see two guys fight? One will throw a punch and the other guy will punch back. Or one throws a knee and the other guy responds with a knee. It is almost as if the first attacker "reminds" the second guy what range and what technique are appropriate. If you hit a guy, it's most likely he is going to hit you right back and his hit will be ten times harder than yours. Women have responded in a way that is immediate and effective. They have knocked instructors unconscious in class.

Our Instructors

Our instructors come from all walks of life. We have women's advocates, social workers, survivors, teachers, high school and college educators, martial arts instructors, and world champions who currently train in arts like Brazilian Jiu-Jitsu, Krav Maga, karate, tae kwon do, JKD, Muay-Thai, and boxing. A kickboxing coach from Kenya and a survivor from the terror attack at the Westgate Mall both traveled eight thousand miles to New York to learn our program.

From Australia, Japan, and Europe and coast to coast in the United States, they all share one thing: a deep desire to empower women with knowledge, information, and tactics that will keep them safe. Most return class after class to continue their education, learn new skills, and receive the most up-to-date safety information available. In addition, we have police agencies from across the country, the U.S. Marine Corps, and the U.S. Air Force.

Defend University Classes and Instructor Certification

At Defend University, our instructor program teaches everyone from advocates with no self-defense experience to professional martial artists to be able to teach this woman-specific reality-based safety and self-defense program to their communities. What makes this program so easy to learn is that the techniques are basic and rely on natural body movements that employ gross motor skills. Our teaching method relies on building new techniques based on something you have already learned. It makes it easier for the technique to be taught by the instructor and easier for the student to absorb and learn. Please visit www.DefendUniversity.com for more information.

GIRLS ON GUARD. This class is the first of two that make up the core program. It is centered on Stranger Encounters and the "Stay with people" principle and covers escaping and defending against the most common sexual assault scenarios, meaning the student will actually learn how to escape from the very same positions in which rapists carry out their attacks. This class is especially effective for attacks by strangers attempting to take you to a secondary location, where you can be victimized, and for defense against the blitz (attacked from behind).

GUARDING OUR GIRLS. This class centers on the Acquaintance Encounter and the "Go to people" principle and is probably the class most often taught in high schools and universities by instructors. The class covers date rape scenarios and provides the tactics and techniques students need to defend against an attack in a secluded area and to escape to a populated one. It is designed to defend against attacks that can be perpetrated by acquaintances, and considering that a majority of all attacks are committed by someone who knows you, this class is one of the most practical.

DEFENSE AGAINST WEAPONS (DAW). This class is focused on the inclusion of weapons. Once students complete the Girls on Guard and Guarding Our Girls classes, we now introduce a variety of weapons to many positions to stop bludgeoning, stabbing, strangling, and/or shooting.

WEAPONS FOR WOMEN. This class is designed to teach women how items common to their environment can be utilized as defensive weapons, should the situation arise. Traditional weapons are also covered and various real-life scenarios that have happened to our students and others are played out in reality-based role-playing.

THE REDUCE-THE-ODDS PROGRAM. This class is focused on prevention and risk reduction. Through the process of lecture, video, and discussion, instructors and students will learn about victimology, the target selection process, the predator mindset, the secondary crime scene, date rape drugs, tactics, strategies, risk reduction, alcohol and the role it plays in sexual assault, and more.

To find out more about Defend University and see if there is a class near you, check out www.DefendUniversity.com.

INDEX

Page numbers in *italics* refer to illustrations.

ABOUT THE
AUTHOR

Steve Kardian has spent more than thirty years as a career law enforcement officer. Kardian is a certified New York State/FBI defensive tactics instructor, a general topics instructor, and an expert on criminal behavior. He received a black belt in Kyokushin and holds the rank of third-degree black belt in Gracie Jiu-Jitsu, a rare accomplishment shared by a small group of Americans. Kardian is a partner and director of Defend University, a women's self-defense training program with a presence on campuses and in corporations all over the United States. He lives in Westchester County, New York.